1 UTILITY

Key concepts and terms: the law of diminishing marginal utility, the optimal purchase rule and consumer equilibrium, intuitive derivation of individual demand curves using marginal utility. (3.3)

UTILITY AND DEMAND

Tony Gordon's utility schedule for chewing gum each day		
Quantity consumed (packs)	Total utility (TU) (cents)	Marginal utility (MU) (cents)
1	80	80
2	144	64
3	192	48
4	224	32
5	244	20
6	244	0
7	230	–14

Tony Gordon's demand schedule for chewing gum each day	
Price (cents)	Quantity demanded (packs)
80	1
64	2
48	3
32	4
20	5
0	6

As people consume goods or services they gain satisfaction (termed utility). **Marginal utility** (**MU**) is the change or additions to total utility resulting from consumption of one extra unit of a good or service. **Total utility** (**TU**) is the aggregate satisfaction gained from consuming successive quantities of a good.

As more of a product is consumed (as shown in the table), total satisfaction (total utility) increases but this will be at a decreasing rate. This is known as the **law of diminishing marginal utility**, that is, as more of a good or service is consumed holding all else constant, total utility increases but at a decreasing rate.

From the table we can observe that if a consumer's purchases increase, then the MU will decrease. Therefore if a consumer was to decrease his or her purchases of a product, then MU would increase.

The rational consumer attempting to maximise his or her total utility should purchase more goods until price **(P) equals MU**; this is the **optimum purchase rule**. The individual demand curve is therefore derived from the individual's MU curve, that is, because consumers receive less extra satisfaction as consumption increases they will only buy more if the price falls.

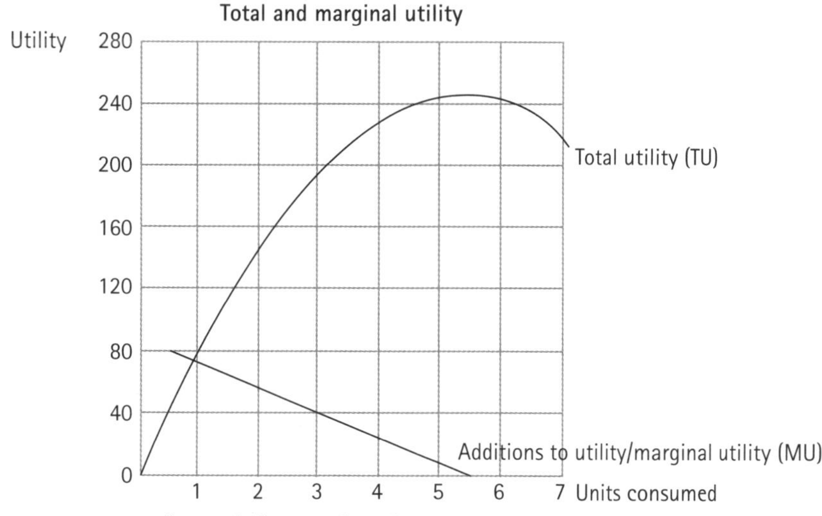

From the graph we can see that while total utility is rising, marginal utility is always positive but beyond the point when total utility is maximised, marginal utility becomes negative. When total utility is at a maximum, marginal utility is zero.

ISBN 9780170241212

EQUI-MARGINAL RULE (A THEORY)

For a consumer aiming to maximise total satisfaction and achieve consumer equilibrium they must satisfy these conditions:

1 spend all their income and
2 the marginal utility per dollar must be equal

i.e., $\frac{MUa}{\text{price a}} = \frac{MUb}{\text{price b}} = \frac{MUc}{\text{price c}}$

In this situation the consumer equilibrium is achieved because the marginal utility of the last dollar spent on each good or service is equal.

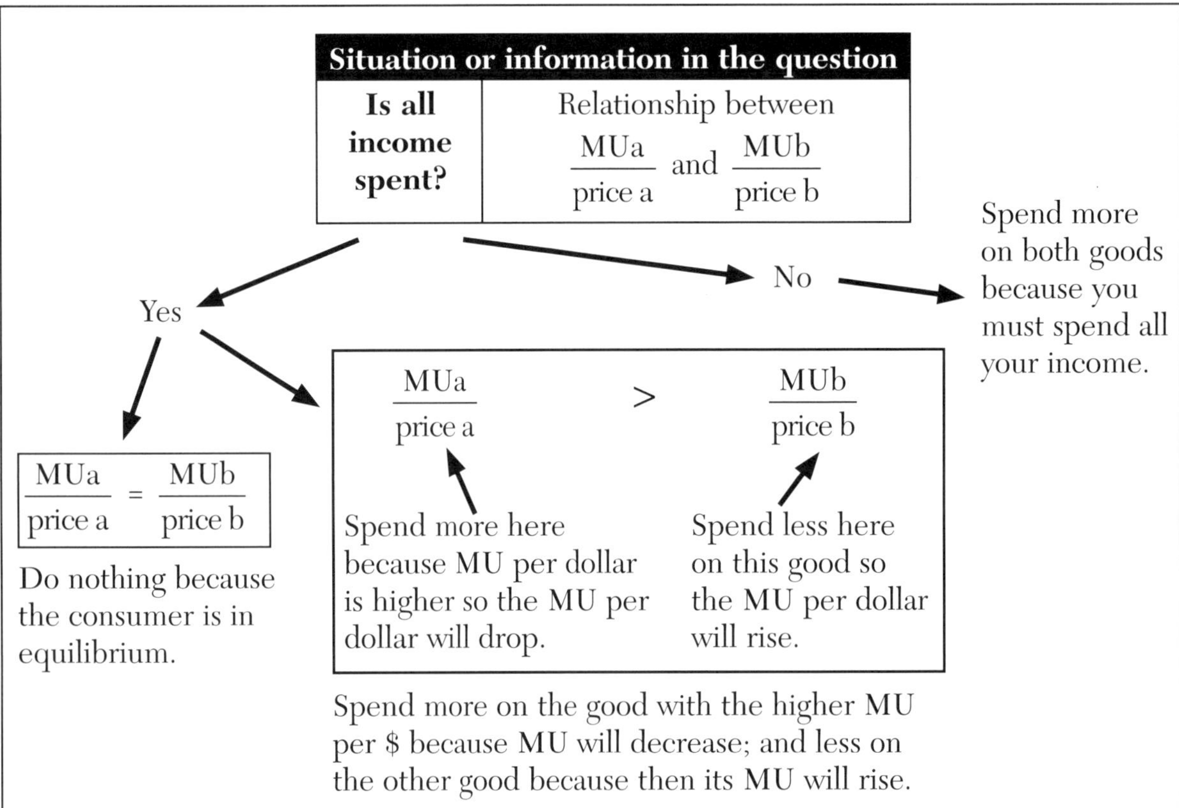

For example, Rangi has $200 to spend and buys 15 of 'x' at $6 and considers the MU of 'x' to be 30. He buys 10 of 'y' at $11 and considers the MU of 'y' to be 55. How can he maximise his total satisfaction?

1 Has Rangi spent all his $200 income? Yes

because	15 of 'x' at $6 =	90
and	10 of 'y' at $11 =	110
		$ 200

2 Does $\frac{MUa}{\text{price a}} = \frac{MUb}{\text{price b}}$? Yes

because $\frac{30}{6} = \frac{55}{11}$

i.e. $5 = 5$

Rangi has satisfied the conditions to maximise satisfaction, he should do nothing.

If Sam purchased the same quantities as Rangi and considered the marginal utilities of the products to be the same but had $220 to spend, he has not maximised his satisfaction because he has not spent all his income, so must spend more on both goods.

Maria has $50 to spend and buys 20 of 'a' at $1 and 15 of 'b' at $2. She considers the MU of 'a' to be 8 and the MU of 'b' to be 12. She meets the first condition of spending all her income of $50 but her MU per dollar are not equal.

Maria has spent all her $50 income because: 20 of 'a' at $1 = $20
15 of 'b' at $2 = $30
$50

Does $\frac{MUa}{\text{price a}} = \frac{MUb}{\text{price b}}$? No

$\left(\frac{8}{1} \neq \frac{12}{2}\right)$

Maria should buy more of 'a' since it has the higher MU per dollar and less of 'b'.

ISBN 9780170241212

NELSON
CENGAGE Learning

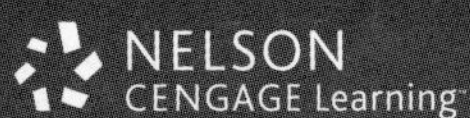

New House

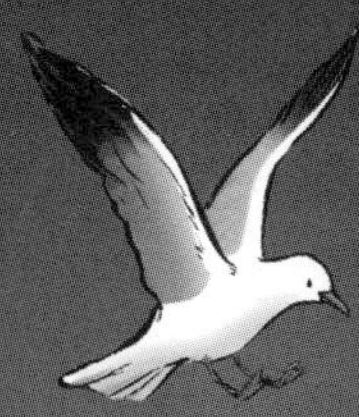

UNDERSTANDING ECONOMICS

For NCEA Level THREE | INTERNAL
MICRO-ECONOMIC CONCEPTS

Skills and Activities for the Key Competencies

Dan Rennie

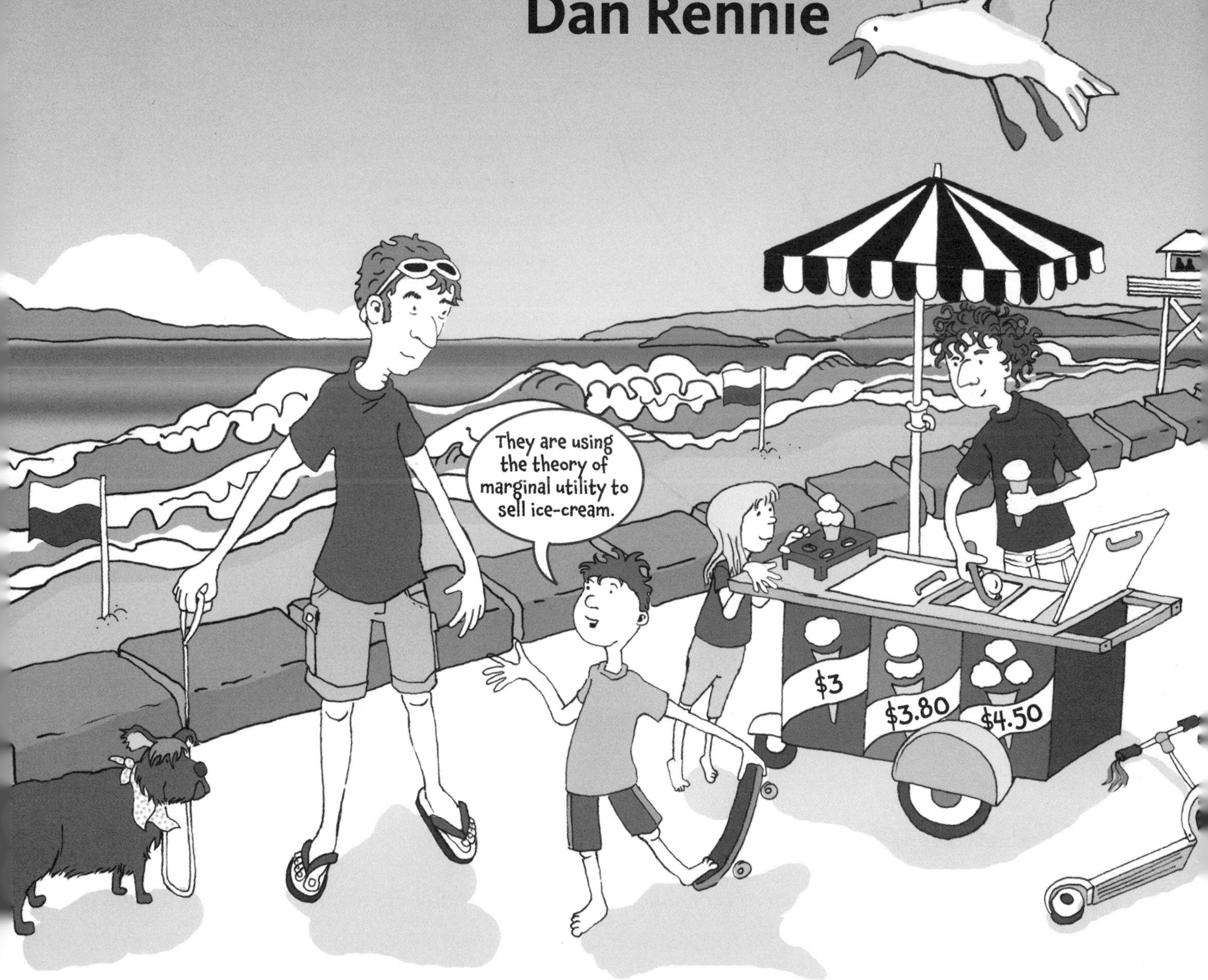
They are using the theory of marginal utility to sell ice-cream.
$3
$3.80
$4.50

Understanding Economics for NCEA Level Three: Micro-economic concepts
1st Edition
Dan Rennie

Typeset by *Book*NZ

Any URLs contained in this publication were checked for currency during the production process. Note, however, that the publisher cannot vouch for the ongoing currency of URLs.

Acknowledgements
Thank you to the following who assisted in various ways to make this publication possible:
- my family - Sue, Nicole, Jacob and Brooke.
- Jane for her typing
- Sally for proof reading

National Library of New Zealand Cataloguing-in-Publication Data
Rennie, Dan, 1959-
Understanding economics NCEA level three. Micro-economic concepts / Dan Rennie.
ISBN 978-017024-121-2
1. Economics. 2. Economics—Problems, exercises, etc.
I. Title.
330.076—dc 23

Cengage Learning Australia
Level 7, 80 Dorcas Street
South Melbourne, Victoria Australia 3205

Cengage Learning New Zealand
Unit 4B Rosedale Office Park
331 Rosedale Road, Albany, North Shore 0632, NZ

For learning solutions, visit **cengage.com.au**

Printed in Singapore by 1010 Printing Group Limited.
6 7 18 17

Contents

Preface

Demonstrate understanding of micro-economic concepts is a stand-alone text and workbook designed to cover aspects of Achievement Standard 3.3.

Key terms and ideas

Utility means satisfaction
Consumers aim to maximise total satisfaction
As more cans are consumed the MU decreases

Zoe's utility schedule for cans of drink (per day)		
Cans consumed	Total utility (cents)	Marginal utility (cents)
1	100	100
2	180	80
3	230	50
4	240	10

Zoe's demand schedule for cans of drink (per day)	
Price (cents)	Quantity demanded (cans)
100	1
80	2
50	3
10	4

Law of diminishing marginal utility	As more of a good/service is consumed, the total utility (satisfaction) will increase at a decreasing rate (i.e., marginal utility will decrease).
Optimum purchase rule	A consumer desiring to maximise total utility should purchase more goods and services until price equals marginal utility (P = MU).
Explaining why MU leads to the downwards sloping demand curve	As consumption increases, MU decreases. The rational consumer attempting to maximise his/her satisfaction will be prepared to purchase to where P = MU. Consumers will only purchase additional units at a lower price. The individual demand curve is therefore derived from the individual MU curve.
Equi-marginal rule Consumer equilibrium is reached when marginal utility of the last dollar spent on each commodity is equal	(a) (i) must spend all income and (ii) $\frac{MUa}{\text{price a}} = \frac{MUb}{\text{price b}}$ } Solution: Do nothing (b) Not all income spent } Spend more on both goods (c) all income spent $\frac{MUa}{\text{price a}} \neq \frac{MUb}{\text{price b}}$ } Spend more on good with higher MU per \$ and less on other good
Total utility (TU)	The aggregate satisfaction gained from consuming successive quantities of a good.
Marginal utility (MU)	The change in total utility resulting from the consumption of one extra unit of a given commodity.

ISBN 9780170241212

STUDENT NOTES: UTILITY

ISBN 9780170241212

Practise questions and tasks

1 a Explain the difference between total utility and marginal utility.

b Explain the law of diminishing marginal utility.

c Complete the table that shows Ian's total and marginal utility from buying cans of soft drink per week.

Quantity consumed (cans)	Total utility (cents)	Marginal utility (cents)
1	200	
2	360	
3	460	
4		64
5		40

d Use the concept of marginal utility to explain why the demand curve for the product slopes downward.

e Use the information in the table above to complete Ian's demand schedule for cans of soft drink per week and draw a demand curve in the grid provided.

Ian's demand schedule for cans of soft drink per week	
Price (cents)	Quantity demanded

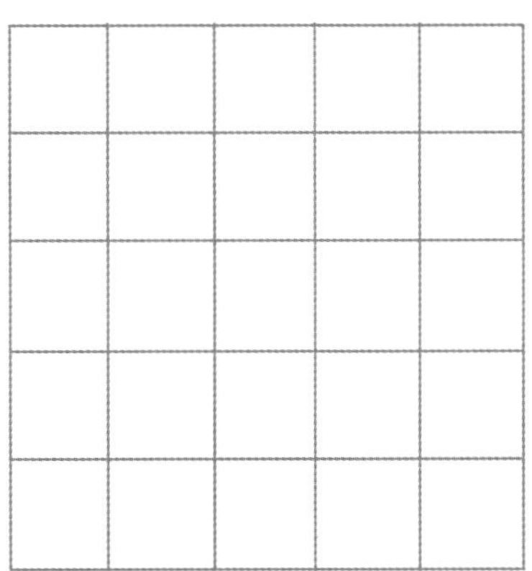

ISBN 9780170241212

2 a Complete the table and use it to complete the sentences.

Quantity consumed (pies)	Total utility	Marginal utility
0	0	
1	24	24
2		20
3	56	
4	60	

A decrease in the amount of a good purchased would ______________ total utility, and marginal utility will ______________.
As more of a product is purchased the marginal utility ______________.

b Look at the values in the marginal utility column above and state the law of economics they show.

____

c State the optimum purchase rule.

____

d State the consumer equilibrium rule (or formula) a consumer should use to ensure they maximise total utility they receive from purchasing two products.

____

____

e The price of good A is $2 and the price of good B is $1.50. If a consumer evaluates the marginal utility of B to be 30 and he or she is in equilibrium with respect to purchases of A and B, then he or she must consider the marginal utility of A to be what?

____

____

f Explain the significance of the law of diminishing marginal utility in deriving the individual demand curve.

____

____

____

g Indicate if the following statements are correct or incorrect.

(i) The consumer gains the maximum utility for the money available when the quantity purchased is at a point where P > MU. ______________

(ii) The consumer gains the maximum utility for the money available when the quantity purchased is at a point where P = MU. ______________

(iii) When a consumer increases consumption of a good or service the MU tends to decrease and they will be prepared to pay less. ______________

(iv) The consumer's equilibrium occurs when the marginal utility per dollar of all goods and services is equal. ______________

ISBN 9780170241212

3 Julian likes to hire videos or video games at the local store. Videos are $10 each and video games $8.

a Complete the table given.

Quantity of each product	Marginal utility of videos (utils)	MU per $ videos	Marginal utility of video games (utils)	MU per $ video games
1	80		56	
2	40		40	
3	20	2	32	
4	10		24	

b State the law of economics that the changing values of marginal utility show in the table.

c State the consumer equilibrium rule Julian needs to apply to maximise the total utility he receives from buying videos and video games.

d How many videos and video games should Julian purchase to maximise his total utility?

Number of videos

Number of video games

e Explain using the optimum purchase rule why Julian would buy fewer videos if their price increased.

ISBN 9780170241212

Review questions

1 Alan is a Year 13 Economics student who likes drinking flavoured milk. Explain the concept of utility. In your answer you should:

- Complete the table below by calculating the missing values.
- Draw Alan's demand schedule for flavoured milk per day in the schedule provided.
- Define the law of diminishing marginal utility.
- Explain, using the law of diminishing marginal utility, why Alan's demand curve will slope downwards to the right. Refer to the table in your answer.

Alan's Utility Schedule for Flavoured Milk (per day)		
Number of bottles consumed	Total utility (cents)	Marginal utility (cents)
1	600	
2	1 000	
3		300
4	1 500	
5		100

ISBN 9780170241212

2 Mark Cambo enjoys hitting golf balls and often goes to the driving range to hit a basket of golf balls. He gives you the following information about his utility.

Explain the concept of utility. In your answer you should:

- Complete the table below by filling in the missing numbers.
- Plot Mark Cambo's demand curve for golf balls on the grid below.
- Name the law that explains why Mark gains less satisfaction with every basket of balls purchased.
- Use marginal utility to explain why Mark Cambo purchases more baskets of golf balls when the price of a basket of golf balls falls.

Mark Cambo's Utility Schedule for baskets of Golf Balls		
Quantity consumed (basket of balls)	Total utility (cents)	Marginal utility (cents)
1	600	
2		400
3	1 200	
4		50

ISBN 9780170241212

3 A consumer, Jacob, assigns the following utility to successive levels of consumption.

Units consumed	Utility					
	Pizza	MU per $	Drink	MU per $	Wedges	MU per $
1	120		22		40	
2	90		20		36	
3	60		18		32	
4	40		14		28	
5	20		12		24	
Price per unit	$10		$2		$4	

Help Jacob maximise the total utility he receives from purchasing pizza, drinks and wedges. In your answer you should:

- Complete the MU per $ column for each product in the table.
- State the consumer equilibrium rule (or formula) Jacob should use to ensure he maximises the total utility he receives.
- Assume Jacob has $20 to spend. What combination of goods will he buy?
- In what order will Jacob purchase pizza, drinks and wedges? Justify your answer for Jacob's fifth purchase.

SELF-EVALUATION REVIEW

Tick (✔) which of the following you know the precise economic answers to (go back and learn those that you have not ticked).

	(✔) TICK
Explain the difference between total and marginal utility.	☐
Explain the law of diminishing utility.	☐
Intuitively derive how the individual demand curve is derived from the individual's marginal utility curve.	☐

ISBN 9780170241212

The size of a firm's operation

Key concepts and terms: apply the law of diminishing returns to show its relationship to increasing costs (3.3).

Diminishing returns

The **law of diminishing returns** refers to the idea that as more and more of a factor (input) is used, with at least one fixed factor, there is some point at which the increase in output will be at a decreasing rate.

In the table, we assume that workers are the only variable factor in the production process. The additions to output (marginal output) increase between the first and second workers. The additions to output reach a maximum on the second worker and thereafter the additional output falls as diminishing returns set in.

Number of workers	Total output	Marginal output
1	10	10
2	30	20
3	40	10
4	46	6
5	48	2
6	46	–2

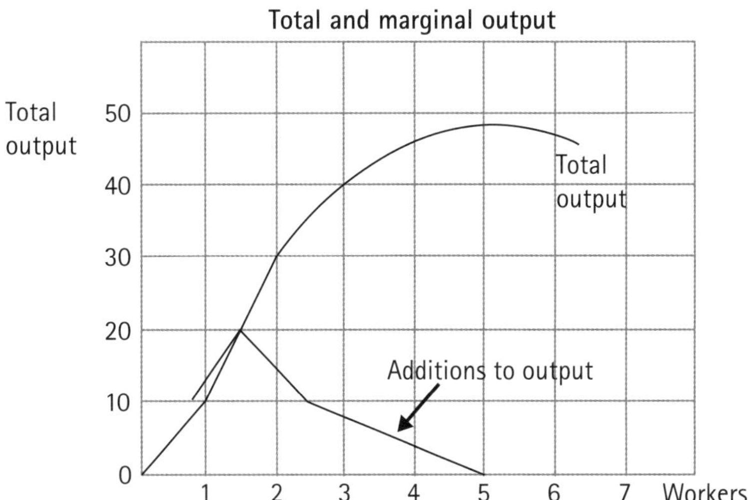

Firms will experience diminishing returns in the short run because, in the short run, at least one factor input is fixed. If additional quantities of other (variable) factors are added into the production process, the total output will increase at a diminishing rate (marginal product must eventually fall). This is because each factor has less of the fixed factor to work with, reducing its ability to produce (extra) output.

Diminishing returns will cause a firm's marginal costs to increase because as each additional variable unit produces less when diminishing returns are occurring, the production of extra units of output will require more and more of variable inputs to produce them (compared with earlier units). Therefore, it follows that the cost of each additional unit produced (i.e., MC) must increase because more inputs are being used to produce it. So, marginal cost must rise as output increases.

Increasing returns to a factor reflect that a firm's short-run average costs would be falling. The increased input of a factor results in increasing additions to output, or a decreased input results in a smaller decrease in output. If a firm decreases an input by 5% but output falls by only 4%, the addition to outputs is actually increasing. The production process must be more efficient than before and costs must be falling (in the short run).

Decreasing returns to a factor (or diminishing returns) reflect that the increase of one input results in decreasing additions to output. The firm increases an input by 5% but output rises by only 3%. Similarly a decrease in an input would result in a larger decrease in output. An input falls by 10% and output decreases by 12%. Both these examples show that the production process has become inefficient. The short-run average costs (**SAC**) will eventually rise.

ISBN 9780170241212

Returns to scale (or factors)

In the long run firms can change all inputs and the firm can be more adaptable and change the size of its operations.

With the increase in size of the firm's operations if the average cost per unit falls, this is known as **economies of scale** or **increasing returns to factors**. An increase in inputs will result in a more than proportionate increase in output.

A firm increases its inputs (the 's' reflects all factors rather than a single input is changed, as is the case in the short run) by 10% and output increases by more than 10%. The firm's long-run average costs (LRAC) must be falling and the production process is efficient.

Economies of scale or increasing returns to factors may be due to existing or new machinery being more efficiently utilised. Also, as output increases, fixed costs are spread over a greater number of units of output. As these average fixed costs fall they will tend to pull down long-run average costs. A firm that is buying in bulk is possibly able to negotiate preferential terms (discounts), and financial economies are possible because large firms may receive lower rates of interest on funds borrowed.

Diseconomies of scale or decreasing returns to factors are possible. The increase in the size of the firm's operation may see cost per unit rise as the inputs combinations used in the production process become less and less efficient. These diseconomies would be illustrated with the long-run average costs rising. An increase in inputs results in a smaller increase in output, for example inputs increase by 10% and output increases by 8%. Similarly if a decrease in inputs results in a larger decrease in output, this reflects that the production process is less efficient and costs per unit are increasing. As inputs decrease by 20% the output decreases by more than 20%.

Graph showing the firm's long-run average costs

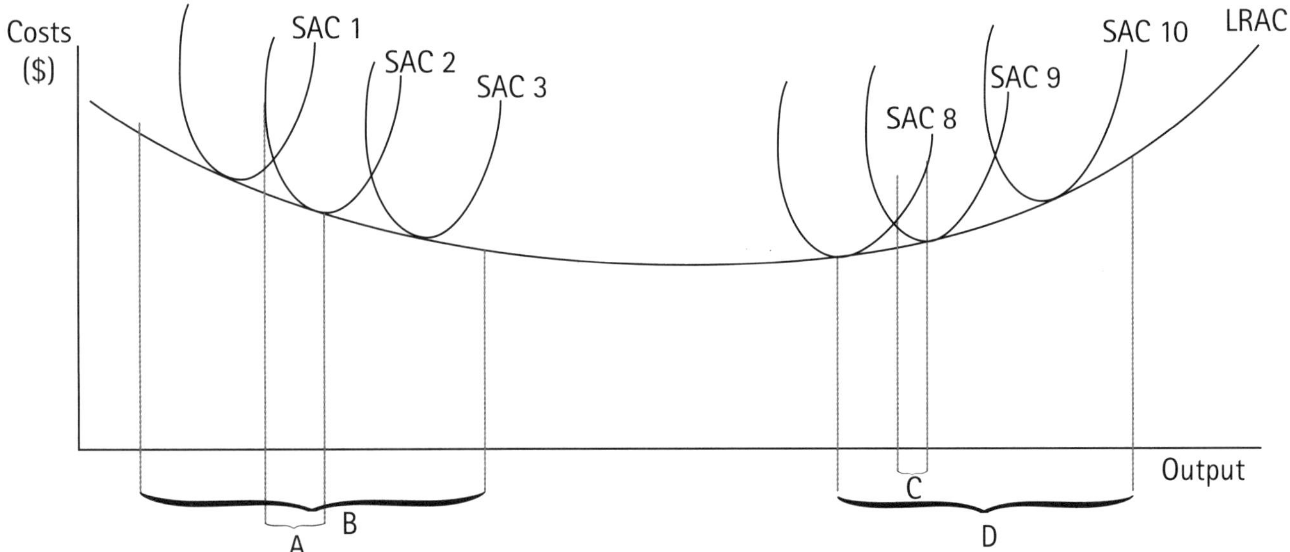

Position	Description
A	SAC falling, increasing returns to a factor
B	LRAC falling, economies of scale
C	SAC rising, diminishing returns
D	LRAC rising, diseconomies of scale

ISBN 9780170241212

Key terms and ideas

Diminishing returns	Occurs in the short-run when there is at least one fixed input; the additions to output at some stage start to decrease.
Why firms experience diminishing returns in the short run	In the short-run, at least one factor input is fixed. If additional quantities of other (variable) factors are added into the production process, the total output will increase at a diminishing rate (marginal product must eventually fall). This is because each factor has less of the fixed factor to work with, reducing its ability to produce (extra) output.
Why diminishing returns cause a firm's marginal costs to increase	As each additional variable unit produces less when diminishing returns are occurring, the production of extra units of output will require more and more of variable inputs to produce them (compared with earlier units). Therefore, it follows that the cost of each additional unit produced (i.e., MC) must increase because more inputs are being used to produce it. So, marginal cost must rise as output increases.
Increasing returns to a factor	A firm's short-run average costs are falling (efficient output-to-input change). This means that an increase in input causes a larger increase in output; or that a decrease in input causes a smaller decrease in output.
Diminishing returns or decreasing returns to a factor	A firm's short-run average costs are rising (inefficient input-to-output change). This means that an increase in input causes a smaller increase in output; or that a decrease in input causes a larger decrease in output.
Economies of scale or increasing returns to factors (scale)	Is when a firm's long-run average cost curve is falling (efficient change of inputs to outputs). This means that an increase in inputs causes a more than proportionate increase in output; or that a decrease in inputs causes a less than proportionate decrease in output.
Diseconomies of scale or decreasing returns to factors (scale)	Is when a firm's long-run average cost curve is rising (inefficient change of inputs to output). This means that a decrease in inputs causes a more than proportionate decrease in output; or that an increase in inputs causes a less than proportionate increase in output.

ISBN 9780170241212

Student notes: Diminishing returns

ISBN 9780170241212

PRACTISE QUESTIONS AND TASKS

1 a Explain why firms experience diminishing returns in the short run.

b Explain why diminishing returns cause a firm's marginal costs to increase.

c For each table indicate when diminishing returns sets in (i) after the ... (ii) with the ....

Output	10	100	250	450	550
Machines	1	2	3	4	5

(i) after the ______________ (ii) with the ______________

Workers	1	2	3	4	5
Total output	5	15	40	90	120

(i) after the ______________ (ii) with the ______________

Output	20	50	90	150	250	260	265
Workers	1	2	3	4	5	6	7

(i) after the ______________ (ii) with the ______________

Machine	Output
1	50
2	150
3	160
4	165
5	167

(i) after the ______________ (ii) with the ______________

ISBN 9780170241212

2 a Why does the marginal cost curve initially fall and then rise?

b Explain why firms experience diminishing returns in the short run.

c Explain why diminishing returns cause a firm's marginal costs to increase.

d (i) Complete the table below by calculating the missing numbers. **Note:** Factory workers are paid $10 per hour.

Table 2: Productivity of Workers at a Golf Club Set Producing Firm			
Total Output (Number of golf club sets)	Total hours worked	Hours required to increase output by one unit	Marginal cost of producing extra units
1	10		
2	15	5	$50
3	40		$250
4	70	30	
5	110		

(ii) At which output level in the table do diminishing returns start? ____________

(iii) Explain why diminishing returns cause the marginal cost of golf club sets production to rise.

ISBN 9780170241212

Review questions

Output	200	300	400	500	600
Marginal costs	30	25	60	78	100

1 Explain the relationship between ouput and marginal costs. In your answer you should:

- Draw a sketch diagram of a marginal cost curve and explain its shape.
- Explain why diminishing returns cause a firm's marginal costs to increase.
- Describe the relationship between marginal cost and the quantity supplied of a product by a firm.

ISBN 9780170241212

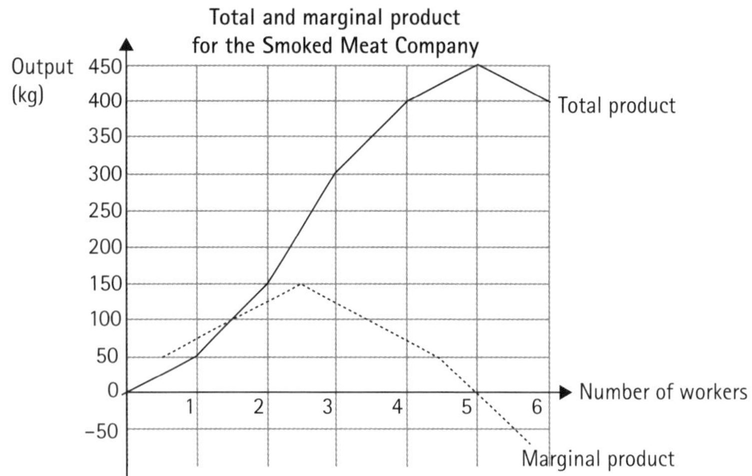

2 Explain the relationship between diminishing returns and a firm's marginal costs. In your answer you should

- State when diminishing returns set in.
- Explain why firms experience diminishing returns in the short run.
- Explain why diminishing returns cause a firm's marginal costs to increase.

SELF-EVALUATION REVIEW

Tick (✔) which of the following you know the precise economic answers to (go back and learn those that you have not ticked).

	(✔) TICK
Can define diminishing returns.	☐
Can identify when diminishing returns set in.	☐
Can distinguish between increasing returns to a factor, economies of scale, diminishing returns and diseconomies of scale	☐

ISBN 9780170241212

3 BREAK–EVEN AND SHUTDOWN

Key concepts and terms: shutdown, break-even, the shape of the marginal cost curve and supply for the perfect competitor (3.3).

BREAK-EVEN AND SHUTDOWN POINTS FOR A FIRM

Break-even is the price at which revenue covers all economic costs. On the graph the value of break-even is shown as the value of Pb. The value of break-even position is at the price $7. The two cost curves equal to the price at the breakeven point are MC and AC.

Shutdown is the price where revenue just covers variable costs. The firm will cease operations and use no variable inputs. Fixed costs will still have to be paid but from some other source. Shutdown is shown as the value Ps on the graph. The shutdown point is at a level where price is just equal to average variable costs (AVC). At this point the firm is indifferent to whether it continues to produce or shuts down. The value of shutdown position is at the price $5. The two cost curves equal to the price at the shutdown point are MC and AVC.

Between the shutdown and break-even points (that is, between Pb and Ps), the firm covers all its variable costs and some of the revenue it makes contributes towards its fixed costs. The firm will continue operating because if it shuts down it will still have to pay all its fixed costs.

At any revenue (or price) below shutdown, the firm fails to cover all its variable costs and will save these costs by not producing.

Break-even and shutdown points

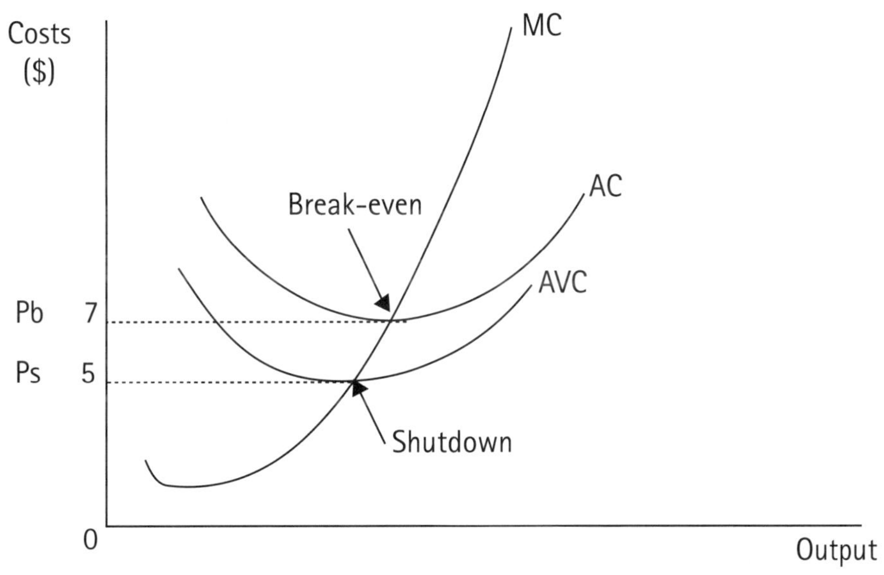

ISBN 9780170241212

Deriving the supply curve from the marginal cost curve

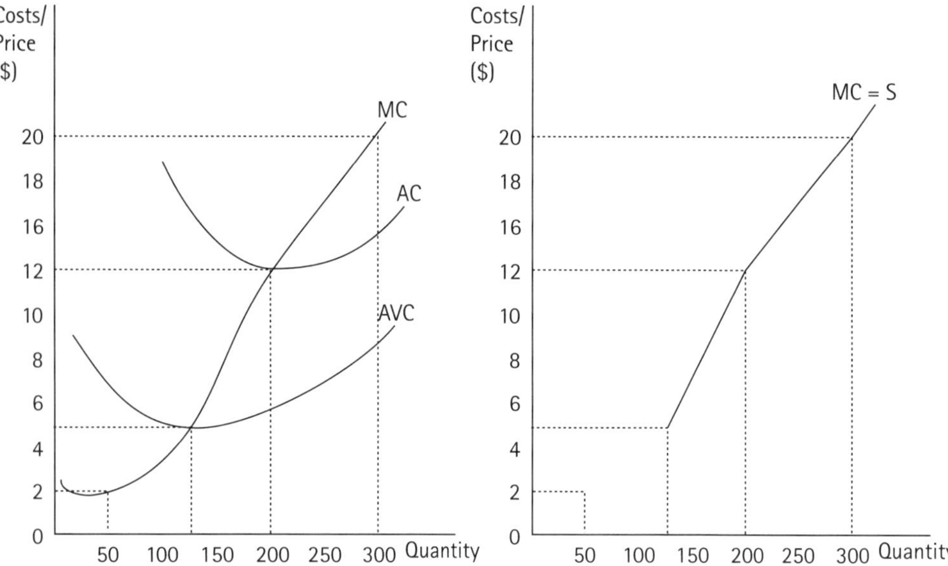

Supply schedule from the MC curve	
Price ($)	Quantity Supplied
2	0
5	125
12	200
20	300

A firm's supply curve is drawn as *that part of MC above AVC (or shutdown).*

At \$2 quantity supplied is zero (0) because the supply curve is derived from MC above AVC (or shutdown). The firm's supply curve is derived from the MC curve and it starts from the minimum of the AVC.

Since a firm's supply curve is the MC curve, it will shift to the right if costs decrease or shift to the left if costs increase.

Key terms and ideas

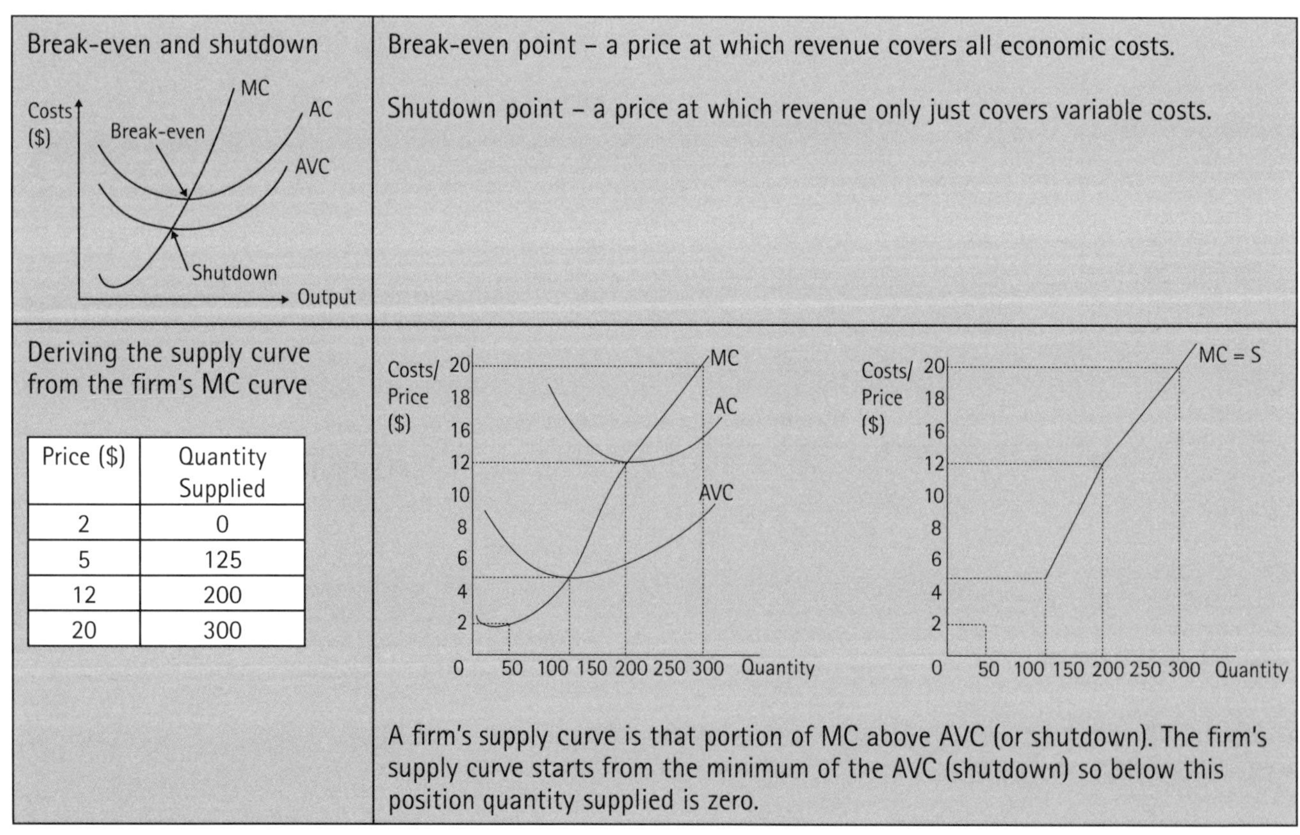

Break-even and shutdown

Break-even point – a price at which revenue covers all economic costs.

Shutdown point – a price at which revenue only just covers variable costs.

Deriving the supply curve from the firm's MC curve

Price ($)	Quantity Supplied
2	0
5	125
12	200
20	300

A firm's supply curve is that portion of MC above AVC (or shutdown). The firm's supply curve starts from the minimum of the AVC (shutdown) so below this position quantity supplied is zero.

ISBN 9780170241212

Student notes: Break-even and shutdown

ISBN 9780170241212

Practise questions and tasks

1 Use the diagram to answer the questions below.

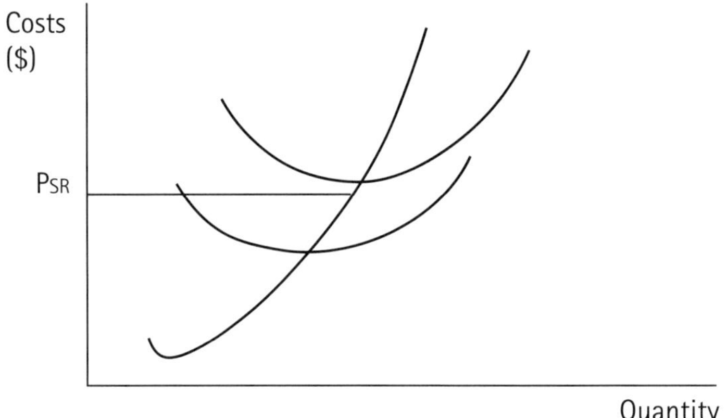

a Label the curves and identify and label the break-even and shutdown points.

b (i) What is the vertical distance between AC and AVC equal to? ____________

(ii) Is this gap a constant? ____________

c (i) When the firm is not producing it must still pay what types of costs? ____________

(ii) What costs are directly related to production? ____________

(iii) If the firm is not producing, what is the value of these costs? ____________

d Write *fixed costs* or *variable costs* for the following terms.

Rent	____________	Wages	____________
Raw materials	____________	Debt servicing	____________
Interest	____________		

e What is debt servicing?

____

____

f Define the following terms.

Break-even: ____________

Shutdown: ____________

g Complete this statement.

If a firm ceases its operation it must still pay ____________ costs. If market price is above the level of average variable cost, it can cover its ____________ costs and still have something left over to pay its fixed costs, it may as well ____________ operating. If price falls below AVC, there is nothing left over to contribute to ____________ costs and variable costs are not fully covered, then the firm should ____________.

ISBN 9780170241212

2 a Write if the following statements are *correct* or *incorrect*.

(i) A firm's supply curve is equal to its AC curve. ____________________

(ii) A firm's supply curve is equal to its MC curve above AVC. ____________________

(iii) When revenue covers all economic costs it is at shutdown. ____________________

(iv) Break-even is when revenue covers variable costs only. ____________________

(v) At any revenue below shutdown, the firm will save paying variable costs by not operating but will still have to pay fixed costs. ____________________

(vi) Break-even is when revenue covers all economic costs. ____________________

b Label the curves on the diagram and clearly label the break-even point (label B) and the shutdown point (label SD).

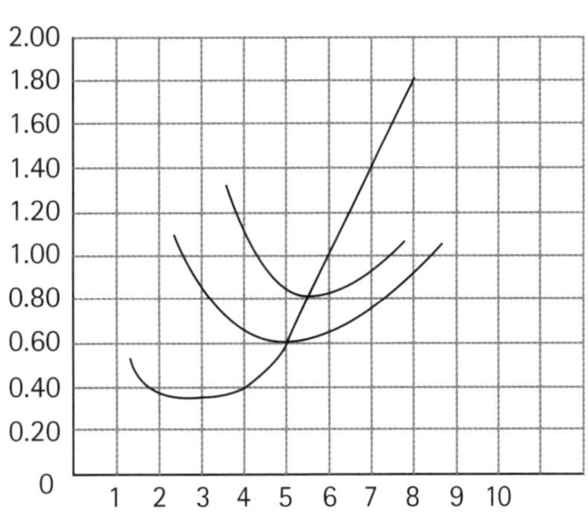

c Give the value of: (i) Shutdown ____________________ (ii) Break-even ____________________.

d What cost concept is represented by the vertical gap between AVC and AC? ____________________

e Why does this gap narrow as output rises?

____

____

____

f Which two cost curves are equal to the price at:

(i) shutdown point? ____________________ (ii) break-even point? ____________________.

g Explain why the firm can continue producing in the short run at $0.70.

____

____

____

ISBN 9780170241212

Review questions

1 A firm's supply curve is the same as its marginal cost curve.

Discuss the relationship between marginal cost and a firm's supply. In your answer you should:

- Define individual supply and marginal cost.
- Explain how marginal cost affects the quantity a producer is willing to supply.
- Explain any difference that exists between the supply curve and the marginal cost curve of a firm.

ISBN 9780170241212

2 The average variable cost curve is important in determining the short-run supply curve for the perfectly competitive producer.

Explain the relationship between a firm's average variable cost curve and its supply curve. In your answer you should:

- Label the curves in Graph one and complete the supply schedule next to it.
- Label the shutdown point (label S) and break-even point (label B) on Graph one.
- Define the terms break-even and shutdown and indicate which two cost curves are equal to the price at each point.
- Explain how a firm's supply curve is derived from MC.

Graph one

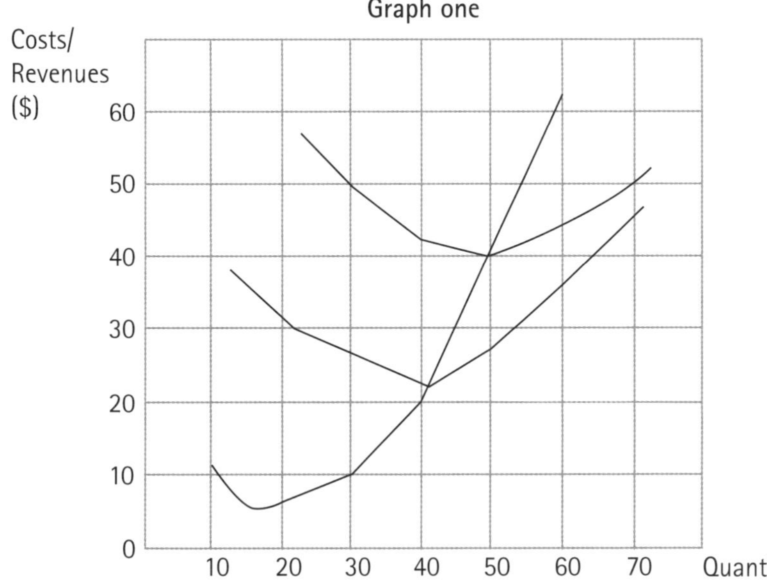

Supply schedule	
Price ($)	
10	
20	
30	
40	
50	
60	

Self-evaluation review

Tick (✔) which of the following you know the precise economic answers to (go back and learn those that you have not ticked).

	(✔) TICK
Identify the shutdown and break-even points.	☐
Define shutdown and break-even.	☐

ISBN 9780170241212

4 Price elasticity of demand, Ep

Key concepts and terms: price elasticity of demand, calculation of price elasticity of demand, reasons for differing elasticities, significance for firms in their pricing decisions (3.3).

Price elasticity of demand

Price elasticity of demand (Ep) measures the *responsiveness of quantity demanded of a good or service to changes in its price.*

To calculate price elasticity of demand we divide the percentage change in quantity demanded by the percentage change in price.

Percentage change method

$$Ep = \frac{\%\Delta QD}{\%\Delta P}$$

where

- Ep = coefficient of price elasticity of demand
- %ΔQD = percentage change in quantity demanded
- %ΔP = percentage change in price

Note the final number (coefficient) will always be a negative number because price and quantity demanded always occur in opposite directions. To be strictly accurate the coefficient should be written as a negative number. However, it is common practice in economics to ignore the negative sign.

When Ep > 1 the price elasticity of demand is termed elastic.
When Ep = 1 the price elasticity of demand is termed unitary.
When Ep < 1 the price elasticity of demand is termed inelastic.

For example: As the price of the product fell by 20% the quantity demanded rose 25%.

$$Ep = \frac{\%\Delta QD}{\%\Delta P} = \frac{25\%}{-20\%} = -1.25 = 1.25 \text{ elastic}$$

Price elasticity of demand can also be calculated by using the midpoint method. The midpoint method is explained below.

Midpoint method

$$Ep = \frac{\left(\frac{\text{change in quantity demanded}}{\text{midpoint of quantity demanded}}\right)}{\left(\frac{\text{change in price}}{\text{midpoint of the prices indicated}}\right)} = \frac{\left(\frac{\Delta Q}{\frac{Q1 + Q2}{2}}\right)}{\left(\frac{\Delta P}{\frac{P1 + P2}{2}}\right)}$$

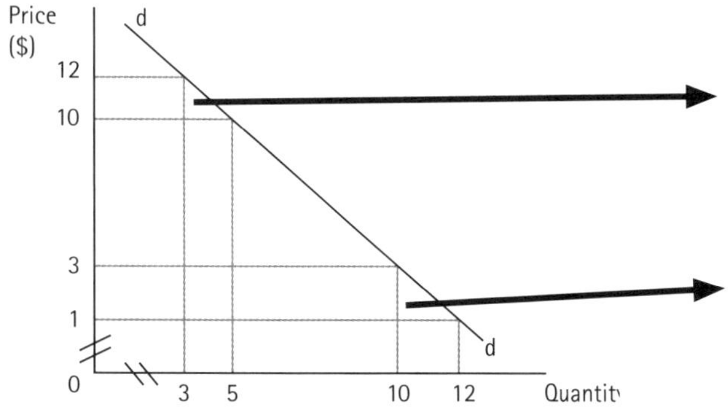

Price ($)
12
10
3
1
0
3 5 10 12 Quantity
d
d

$$Ep = \frac{(2/4)}{(-2/11)} = -2.75 = 2.75 \text{ elastic}$$

$$Ep = \frac{(-2/11)}{(2/2)} = -0.18 = 0.18 \text{ inelastic}$$

Price elasticity of demand is a point concept so a single demand curve can have a range of elasticities, typically relatively elastic at the top end and relatively inelastic at the lower end.

ISBN 9780170241212

In extreme cases, slope does indicate elasticity.

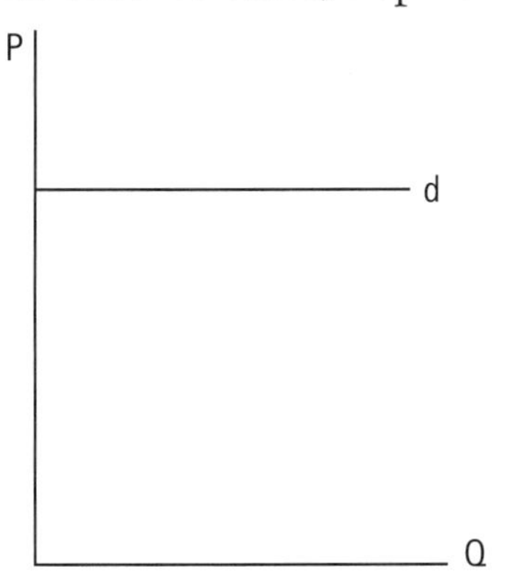

Perfectly (or infinitely) elastic – a horizontal curve, Ep = ∞

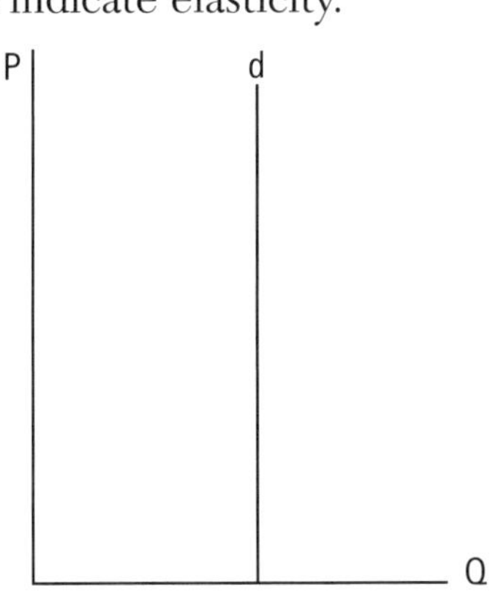

Perfectly inelastic (zero elasticity) – a vertical curve, Ep = 0

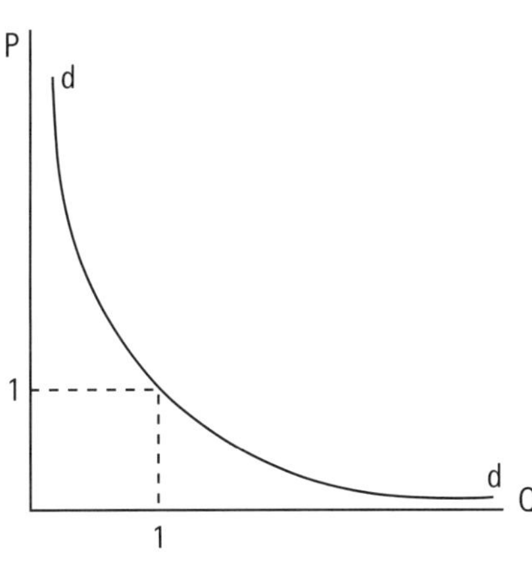

Unit elasticity – rectangular hyperbola, Ep = 1

Price elasticity of demand can also be calculated using the revenue method, which compares the change in **price (P)** with the change in **total revenue (TR)**. Total revenue (TR) equals **price (P)** times **quantity (Q)**. The table gives a summary of elasticity using the revenue method.

	Price and total revenue relationship	Elasticity
P ↕; TR remains unchanged	Any change in price will see total revenue remain the same	Unitary
P ↑; TR ↑ or P ↓; TR ↓	Price and total revenue changes are in the same direction	Inelastic
P ↑; TR ↓ or P ↓; TR ↑	Price and total revenue changes are in the opposite direction	Elastic

For example

Unitary elasticity (Ep = 1)

Any change in price results in no change in total revenue.

Price (P) $	Quantity demanded (Q)	Total revenue (TR) $
25	4	100
20	5	100

Inelastic demand (Ep < 1)

When price increases so will total revenue and if price decreases so will total revenue. Changes in price and total revenue move in the same direction. In the example shown, as price increases from 60 cents to 80 cents, total revenue increases from $6.00 to $7.20, so Ep is inelastic.

Price (P) $	Quantity demanded (Q)	Total revenue (TR) $
60c	10	$6.00
80c	9	$7.20

Elastic demand (Ep > 1)

When price increases total revenue will decrease or if price decreases then total revenue will increase. When the changes in price and total revenue are in opposite directions, so Ep is elastic. As price decreases from $12 to $10 the total revenue increases from $1,200 to $1,300.

Price (P) $	Quantity demanded (Q)	Total revenue (TR) $
$12	100	$1 200
$10	130	$1 300

ISBN 9780170241212

Factors that determine elasticity of demand

Inelastic demand includes products that tend to have no or few close substitutes and are often considered necessities such as bread, milk, medical services. The products may be addictive such as cigarettes or alcohol. When the relative cost of the commodity is a small fraction of total outlay then the demand will be inelastic, for example a newspaper.

Products that have **elastic demand** have many substitutes and are often considered luxuries such as fashion clothing and cars because there are substitutes such as walking, catching a bus, etc.

Application of elasticity

When price elasticity of demand is less than one, this means that a given change in price causes a less than proportionate change in quantity demanded and indicates inelastic demand.

When price elasticity of demand is greater than one, this means that a given change in price causes a more than proportionate change in quantity demanded and indicates elastic demand.

If a firm desires to increase revenue it would increase price if the product was inelastic in nature and decrease price if the product was elastic in nature.

Government will raise more revenue from taxes on products that are inelastic in nature such as cigarettes and beer.

The incidence of a tax will fall more heavily on the consumer if demand is inelastic and more on the producer when demand is elastic.The incidence of the tax refers to who actually pays the tax.

Key terms and ideas

Price elasticity of demand (Ep)	Measures the responsiveness of quantity demanded of a good or service to changes in its price
Formula to calculate price elasticity of demand midpoint method (Ep > 1 is elastic Ep = 1 is unitary Ep < 1 is inelastic)	$Ep = \dfrac{\left(\dfrac{\text{change in quantity demanded}}{\text{midpoint of quantity demanded}}\right)}{\left(\dfrac{\text{change in price}}{\text{midpoint of the prices indicated}}\right)} = \dfrac{\left(\dfrac{\Delta Q}{\frac{Q1 + Q2}{2}}\right)}{\left(\dfrac{\Delta P}{\frac{P1 + P2}{2}}\right)}$
Price elasticity of demand using the revenue method	TR remains unchanged when the price changes, Ep = 1 TR and price changes occur in the same direction, e.g., P ↓ TR ↓, Ep < 1 TR and price changes occur in opposite directions, e.g., P ↑ TR ↓, Ep > 1
Inelastic demand	A given change in price causes a less than proportionate change in quantity demanded.
Elastic demand	A given change in price causes a more than proportionate change in quantity demanded.
Features of goods and services that are inelastic in nature	Addictive, few substitutes, often considered necessities, e.g., food, cigarettes. The incidence of a sales tax falls more on the consumer. Takes a small proportion of total income spent.
Features of goods and services that are elastic in nature	Many substitutes, often considered luxuries, e.g. cars, meals out. Incidence of a tax will fall more on the producer. Takes a high proportion of total income spent.

ISBN 9780170241212

Student notes: Price elasticity of demand

ISBN 9780170241212

Practise questions and tasks

1 a Define price elasticity of demand and give the formula to calculate Ep.

b Work out price elasticity of demand for each question below. Show your working (round to two decimal places). Use the midpoint method.

(i) The price of coffee rose from $15 per kg to $20 per kg and sales fell from 100 kg to 80 kg per week.

(ii)

Price ($)	Quantity demanded
1.50	100
1.70	95

(iii) Work out the Ep on the curve at the positions indicated.

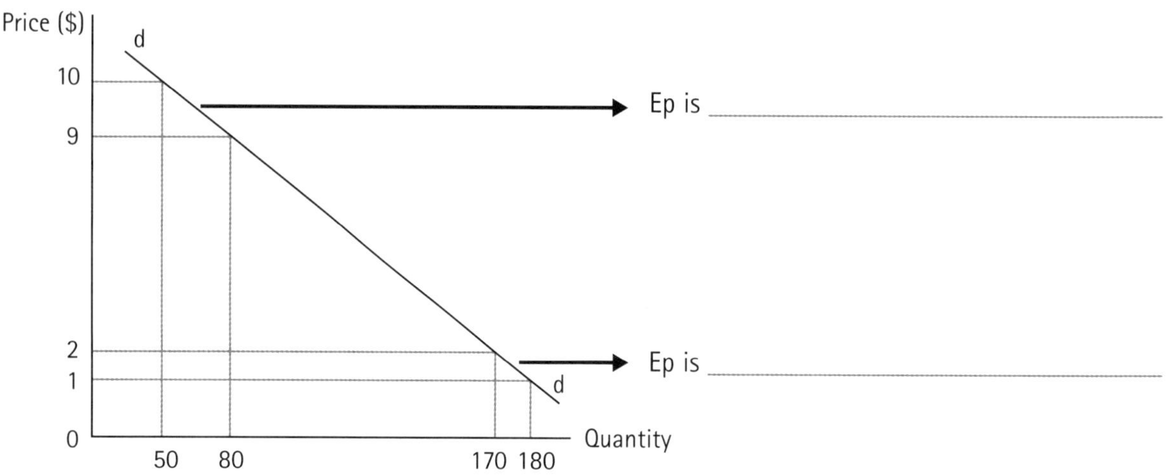

c Complete the table by giving possible explanations for the price elasticity of demand coefficient indicated.

Product (and price elasticity of demand coefficient)	Possible explanations
Toilet paper (0.23)	
New car (2.45)	

ISBN 9780170241212

2 Calculate price elasticity of demand for each of the following questions (to two decimal places). Work out Ep using (i) the midpoint method and (ii) the percentage change method. Show your working.

a

(i) ______________________________

____

(ii) ______________________________

b

	Price $	Quantity demanded
Old situation	25	100
New situation	30	60

(i) ______________________________

____

(ii) ______________________________

c Complete the table.

Relative changes in price/revenue	Elasticity – unitary, inelastic, elastic
(i) Price increases and total revenue remains unchanged	
(ii) Price increases and total revenue increases	
(iii) Total revenue increases when price rises from \$10 to \$12	
(iv) P ↓ TR ↓	
(v) P ↓ TR remains the same	
(vi) Price decreases and total revenue increases	
(vii) TR ↑ when price falls	
(viii) Revenue remains the same when price falls	
(ix) Change in price and total revenue are in the same direction	
(x) TR ↑ P ↑ or P ↓ TR ↓	
(xi) Changes in TR and P go in the opposite direction	

d (i) Give reasons why the price elasticity of demand coefficient of wiper blades is 0.19.

____

____

____

(ii) Indicate what will happen to a firm's revenue if they increase the price. Explain why.

____

____

____

ISBN 9780170241212

3 Indicate the price elasticity of demand indicated by the situation outlined in the table below.

	Situation	Elasticity of demand
a	The response to a given change in price is an exactly proportionate change in quantity demanded	
b	The response to a given change in price is a more than proportionate change in quantity demanded	
c	The response to a given change in price is a less than proportionate change in quantity demanded	
d	A given change in prices evokes a more than proportionate change in quantity demanded	
e	%Δ price < %Δ quantity demanded	
f	%Δ price = %Δ quantity demanded	
g	%Δ QD < %Δ price	

4 Doctor visits fell from 10 000 to 9 000 when price increased from $25 to $30. What is the price elasticity of demand for doctor visits? Give a possible reason for doctor visits, relating it to the Ep you calculated.

5 The brewery decides to increase the price of a jug from $4.50 to $5.00 and the quantity sold decreases from 7 500 to 7 300.

a Work out the change in revenue from the price increase. Was this an increase or decrease in revenue?

b Work out Ep using the midpoint method.

6 a A car firm sells new cars for $25 000 and sells 10 000. What is the revenue made?

b When the price is slashed to $20 000 they sell 13 000. What is the revenue made?

c From this information what is Ep, and at what price would you sell cars for and why?

ISBN 9780170241212

Review questions

1 Price elasticity of demand is a point concept.

Explain price elasticity of demand using the graph below. In your answer you should:

- Define 'price elasticity of demand'.
- Calculate price elasticity of demand along the demand curve. Use the midpoint method and show your working.
- Describe the features of products that are elastic or inelastic in nature.

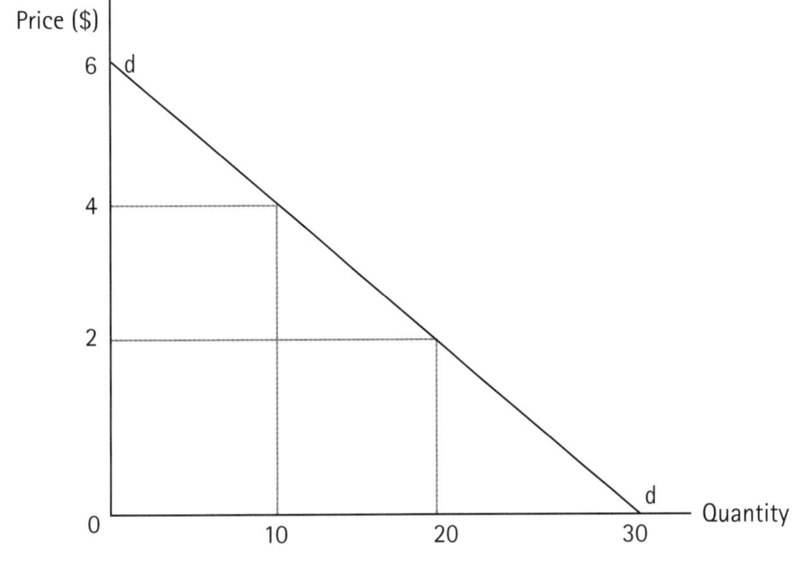

ISBN 9780170241212

2 Various factors determine the price elasticity of demand for a product. The demand coefficient of water is 0.15, coffee 0.56 and meals out at a restaurant 1.35. Firms use this knowledge in their pricing decisions.

Explain factors that determine price elasticity of demand and how firms use this knowledge. In your answer you should:

- Explain factors that influence price elasticity of demand with reference to the information above.
- Explain how firms will use a knowledge of price elasticity of demand in their pricing decisions.

ISBN 9780170241212

3 The price elasticity of demand coefficient of overseas trips is 2.67.

Fully explain the price elasticity of demand for overseas trips. In your answer you should:

- Define price elasticity of demand.
- Explain why the price elasticity of demand for overseas trips is elastic.
- Explain what will happen to the total revenue for producers of overseas trip if the price falls by 4%.

SELF-EVALUATION REVIEW

Tick (✔) which of the following you know the precise economic answers to (go back and learn those that you have not ticked).

	(✔) TICK
Calculate price elasticity of demand either using the midpoint method or relating it to total expenditure.	☐
Recognise the reasons for differing price elasticities of demand for various goods.	☐
Appreciate that some firms will use the concepts of elasticity of demand in their pricing decisions of goods and services.	☐

ISBN 9780170241212

5 Cross elasticity of demand, Ecross and income elasticity of demand, Ey

Key concepts and terms: cross elasticity of demand, calculation of cross elasticity of demand, income elasticity of demand, calculation of income elasticity of demand, significance for firms of income elasticity or cross elasticity of demand (3.3).

Substitutes or complements

Cross elasticity of demand (Ecross) measures the responsiveness of the quantity demanded of one good to changes in the price of another good.

Cross elasticity can be used to understand and classify the relationships between goods and services, it can indicate if products are substitutes or complements simply by the sign of the coefficient. A positive cross elasticity coefficient indicates that the products are substitutes while a negative coefficient indicates they are complements.

The formulas used in calculating cross elasticity of demand are somewhat similar to those used in calculating price elasticity of demand, and are employed following the same principles. Commodities are labelled simply as X and Y (or A and B).

Midpoint method

$$\text{Ecross} = \frac{\left(\dfrac{\text{change in quantity demanded of X}}{\text{midpoint of quantity demanded of X given}}\right)}{\left(\dfrac{\text{change in price of Y}}{\text{midpoint of the prices of Y indicated}}\right)} = \frac{\left(\dfrac{\Delta QX}{\dfrac{QX_1 + QX_2}{2}}\right)}{\left(\dfrac{\Delta PY}{\dfrac{PY_1 + PY_2}{2}}\right)}$$

For example: The purchases of good X increased from 100 to 150 units as the price of good Y decreased from \$100 to \$80.

$$\text{Ecross} = \frac{\left(\dfrac{\text{change in quantity demanded of X}}{\text{midpoint of quantity demanded of X given}}\right)}{\left(\dfrac{\text{change in price of Y}}{\text{midpoint of the prices of Y indicated}}\right)} = \frac{\left(\dfrac{50}{125}\right)}{\left(\dfrac{-20}{90}\right)} = -1.80$$

goods X and Y are complements because the Ecross is a negative coefficient

Percentage change method

$$\text{Ecross} = \frac{\%\Delta QD\ (A)}{\%\Delta P\ (B)}$$

where
- Ecross = coefficient of cross elasticity of demand
- %ΔQD (A) = percentage change in quantity demanded of commodity A
- %ΔP (B) = percentage change in price of commodity B

For example: The price of good B fell by 8% and as a result the purchases of good A decreased by 20%.

$$\text{Ecross} = \frac{\%\Delta QD\ (A)}{\%\Delta P\ (B)} = \frac{-20\%}{-8\%} = +2.50$$

goods A and B are substitutes because the Ecross is a positive coefficient

The size of the coefficient will indicate the strength of the relationship. A coefficient between zero and one denotes weak cross elasticity, while figures greater than 1 imply a close relationship and strong cross elasticity.

ISBN 9780170241212

Substitutes are products that can be used in place of something else, for example, butter in place of margarine, coffee in place of tea, beef in place of lamb. For substitutes a rise in the price of one good and thus an increase in demand for the substitute (alternative) is a positive change. This is shown in the graphs. This is a positive change because price and demand for these products move in the same direction, which means that the products are substitutes.

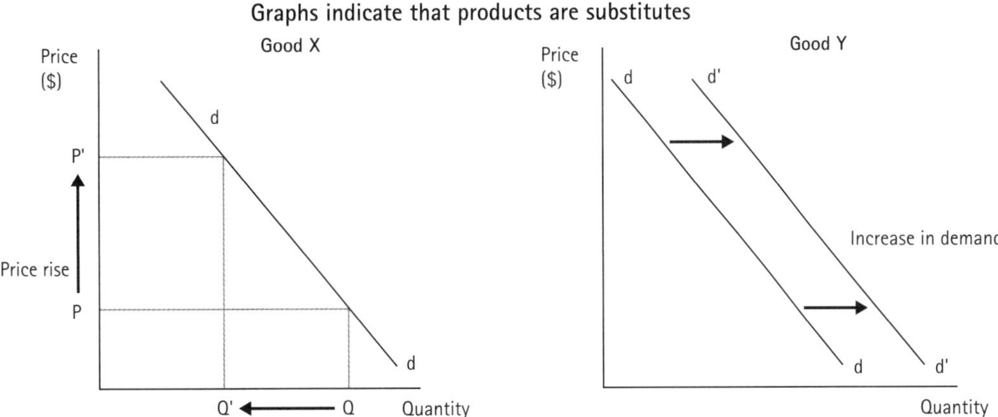

Complements are products that go or are used together, for example, cars and petrol, hot dogs and tomato sauce. For a complement the rise in price of one causes a decrease in demand for the other, a negative change. The effect on graphs is shown below. This is a negative change because price and demand for these products move in opposite directions indicating that the products are complements.

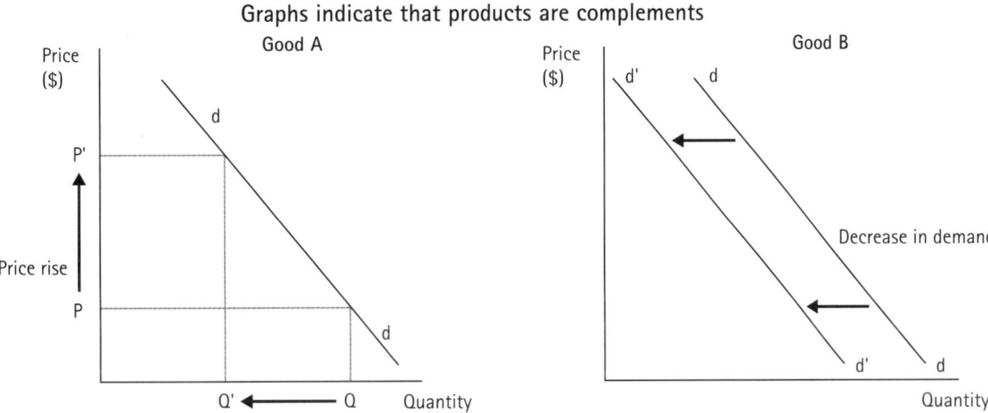

Income elasticity of demand, Ey

Income elasticity of demand (Ey) measures the *responsiveness of quantity demanded to changes in consumer incomes.*

Income elasticity of demand is concerned with the way in which consumer demand responds to a change in income. The coefficient of income elasticity of demand will determine if the good or service is inferior, normal necessities or normal luxuries.

An **inferior good** is a good or service for which the quantity demanded and income changes move in opposite directions, and income elasticity (Ey) is a negative number. We buy less inferior goods and services as our income rises.

A **normal good** is a good or service for which changes in quantity demanded and income move in the same direction, for example if income increases so will quantity demanded. Income elasticity for a normal necessity is greater than zero but less than one; for a normal luxury the income elasticity is greater than one. In both cases, for a normal good the income elasticity is a positive number.

ISBN 9780170241212

To calculate income elasticity of demand we use the following formulas:

Percentage change method

$$Ey = \frac{\%\Delta QD}{\%\Delta Y}$$

where

Ey = income elasticity of demand
%ΔQD = percentage change in quantity demanded
%ΔY = percentage change in consumers' income

For example: Julian's income rises by 4% and the quantity decreases by 10%.

$$Ey = \frac{\%\Delta QD}{\%\Delta Y} = \frac{-10\%}{4\%} = -2.50 \text{ inferior good}$$

Income and quantity changes are in opposite directions so Ey is a negative number.

Midpoint method

$$Ey = \frac{\left(\dfrac{\text{change in quantity demanded}}{\text{midpoint of quantity demanded}}\right)}{\left(\dfrac{\text{change in income}}{\text{midpoint of incomes}}\right)} = \frac{\left(\dfrac{\Delta Q}{\frac{Q1 + Q2}{2}}\right)}{\left(\dfrac{\Delta Y}{\frac{Y1 + Y2}{2}}\right)}$$

For example: Bill's income fell from $200 to $150 and quantity demanded decreases from 50 to 40.

$$Ey = \frac{\left(\dfrac{\text{change in quantity demanded}}{\text{midpoint of quantity demanded}}\right)}{\left(\dfrac{\text{change in income}}{\text{midpoint of incomes}}\right)} = \frac{\left(\dfrac{-10}{45}\right)}{\left(\dfrac{-50}{175}\right)} = 0.78 \text{ normal necessity}$$

Both income and quantity fell for Bill so since these changes are in the same direction, Ey is a positive number which indicates a normal good.

Firms would respond to increasing incomes in a society by producing more normal goods and fewer inferior products. During a recession with falling incomes and people losing jobs, products with high income elasticity of demand (normal luxuries) will be most affected because people will be forced to buy other products (necessities or inferior goods).

KEY TERMS AND IDEAS

Cross elasticity of demand	Measures the responsiveness of quantity demanded of one good to changes in price of another good. Cross elasticity can indicate if goods are substitutes or complements
Substitutes	Ecross is a positive coefficient
Complements	Ecross is a negative coefficient
Income elasticity of demand (Ey)	Measures the responsiveness of quantity demanded to changes in incomes.
Inferior goods	Ey is a negative number. Quantity demanded and income changes are in opposite directions.
Normal goods	Ey is a positive number. Quantity demanded and income changes are in the same direction. If Ey > 1, the commodity is a normal luxury. If 0 < Ey < 1, the commodity is a normal necessity.

ISBN 9780170241212

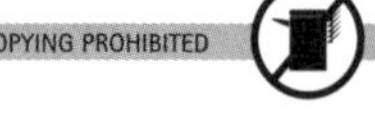

STUDENT NOTES: CROSS ELASTICITY AND INCOME ELASTICITY OF DEMAND

ISBN 9780170241212

Practise questions and tasks

1 a Define 'cross elasticity of demand'.

b What is the purpose of calculating cross elasticity of demand?

c Calculate cross elasticity of demand and indicate if the products are substitutes or complements.
(i) The price of good A increased by 8% and the quantity demanded of good B rose by 5%.

Ecross =

(ii) The price of good A rose from $8 to $12 and in response the purchases for good B decreased from 200 units to 100 units.

Ecross =

2 Work out the income elasticity for each question using the midpoint method and indicate what type of goods they are. Show your working.

a When an individual's disposable income falls from $500 to $450 per week, their purchases of a product increase from 12 to 15.

b

Previous income	$40 000
New income	$50 000
Previous purchases	100
New purchases	120

c

	Quantity demanded	Income ($)
New situation	4	30
Old situation	8	40

ISBN 9780170241212

3 a Define 'income elasticity' and give the formula to calculate Ey.

....

....

....

b Complete the table.

Information	Inferior goods Normal necessities Normal luxuries
(i) Income and quantity demanded changes are in opposite directions	
(ii) Goods have a negative income elasticity of demand	
(iii) Goods have a positive income elasticity of demand	
(iv) Ey < 0	
(v) An increase in incomes leads to an increase in demand (or quantity demanded)	
(vi) Income elasticity of demand is greater than one	
(vii) An increase in income will cause quantity demanded to decrease	
(viii) A drop in income will cause a decrease in demand	
(ix) If a household's income rose from $200 to $250 per week and the quantity demanded rose from 20 to 24	
(x) If a household's income rose from $200 to $250 per week and the quantity demanded fell from 24 to 20	
(xi) The percentage change in income brings about a much larger percentage change in quantity demanded, e.g., laptop computer, cellphones	
(xii) A percentage fall in income causes only a small percentage decrease in quantity demanded, e.g., salt, bread	
(xiii) A percentage rise in income causes a percentage decrease in quantity demanded.	

c Complete the empty spaces in the sentences below.

Income elasticity of demand (Ey) ____________ the ________________ of quantity demanded to ________________________________. Goods and services with a negative income elasticity of demand are classified as ________________. Goods and services with a ________________________________ are classified as normal goods.

ISBN 9780170241212

4 a An economist planned to measure the strength of a possible relationship between increasing diesel prices and the quantity of alternative fuels demanded. Name the elasticity concept that would be used.

b Complete the table by placing a tick (✓) in the column to indicate the cross elasticity of demand coefficient.

Situation	Positive coefficient	Negative coefficient
(i) A rise in the price of one good causes a fall in the quantity of the other good.		
(ii) A rise in the price of one good causes a rise in the quantity of the other good.		
(iii) A fall in the price of one good causes a fall in the quantity of the other good.		

c Define cross elasticity of demand.

5 The consumption of apples declined by 12% and the consumption of oranges declined by 8%. In the same period, the consumption of bananas increased by 6%.
Assume that the prices of apples and oranges rose by 4% over the same period of time.

a (i) Calculate the coefficient for the price elasticity of demand for apples. Show your working.

(ii) Assume that the coefficient calculated in a (i) is correct. What has happened to the total revenue of apple producers?

b (i) Calculate the coefficient for the price elasticity of demand for bananas to a change in price of apples. Show your working.

(ii) What does your answer to b (i) suggest about the relationship between bananas and apples?

ISBN 9780170241212

Review questions

1 Pizzas and gourmet hamburgers are substitutes, while a rented DVD would be considered a complement for either a pizza or gourmet burger.

Explain cross elasticity of demand and price elasticity of demand. In your answer you should:

- Indicate if the cross elasticity of demand for pizzas and gourmet hamburgers is a positive or negative and explain why.
- Explain whether it is a good idea for the firm to raise the price of a good that is inelastic in nature.
- Explain why goods that have no close substitutes have inelastic demand.

ISBN 9780170241212

2 Economists can measure the relationship between prices of one product and demand for another. Explain the concept of cross elasticity of demand. In your answer you should:

- Define cross elasticity of demand and indicate what the cross elasticity coefficient indicates.
- Explain with the aid of a diagram what substitutes are.
- Explain with the aid of a diagram what complements are.

ISBN 9780170241212

3 Income elasticity of demand is used by firms when making decisions.
Explain income elasticity of demand. In your answer you should:

- Explain income elasticity of demand.
- Explain the difference between inferior and normal goods.
- Explain how a firm's knowledge of income elasticity will influence its decision making.

SELF-EVALUATION REVIEW

Tick (✔) which of the following you know the precise economic answers to (go back and learn those that you have not ticked).

	(✔) TICK
Define 'cross elasticity of demand' and calculate cross elasticity of demand and determine if products are substitutes or complements.	☐
Define income elasticity and calculate income elasticity.	☐
Explain the relationship between the level of individual incomes and the type of goods and services they are likely to purchase.	☐

ISBN 9780170241212

6 Price elasticity of supply, Es

Key concepts and terms: price elasticity of supply, calculation of price elasticity of supply, supply responsiveness in the long term compared with the short term (3.3).

Price elasticity of supply (Es) measures the *responsiveness of quantity supplied of a good to changes in price.*

To calculate the coefficient of price elasticity of supply we divide the percentage change in quantity supplied by the percentage change in price. The formula is given below.

Percentage change method

$$Es = \frac{\%\Delta QS}{\%\Delta P}$$

where

Es = coefficient of price elasticity of supply
%ΔQS = percentage change in quantity supplied
%ΔP = percentage change in price

When Es > 1 the price elasticity of supply is termed elastic.
When Es = 1 the price elasticity of supply is termed unitary.
When Es < 1 the price elasticity of supply is termed inelastic.

For example, as the price of the product increased by 8% the quantity supplied increased by 5%.

$$Es = \frac{\%\Delta QS}{\%\Delta P} = \frac{5\%}{8\%} = 0.63 \text{ supply is inelastic}$$

Midpoint method

Price elasticity of supply can be calculated by the midpoint method as shown.

$$Es = \frac{\left(\dfrac{\text{change in quantity supplied}}{\text{midpoint of quantity supplied given}}\right)}{\left(\dfrac{\text{change in price}}{\text{midpoint of the prices indicated}}\right)} = \frac{\left(\dfrac{\Delta Qs}{\frac{Q1 + Q2}{2}}\right)}{\left(\dfrac{\Delta P}{\frac{P1 + P2}{2}}\right)}$$

For example, at a price of \$110 quantity supplied is 500, while at a price of \$90 quantity supplied is 300.

$$Es = \frac{\left(\dfrac{\text{change in quantity supplied}}{\text{midpoint of quantity supplied given}}\right)}{\left(\dfrac{\text{change in price}}{\text{midpoint of the prices indicated}}\right)} = \frac{\left(\frac{200}{400}\right)}{\left(\frac{20}{100}\right)} = 2.50 \quad \text{supply is elastic}$$

In extreme cases slope will indicate the price elasticity of supply.

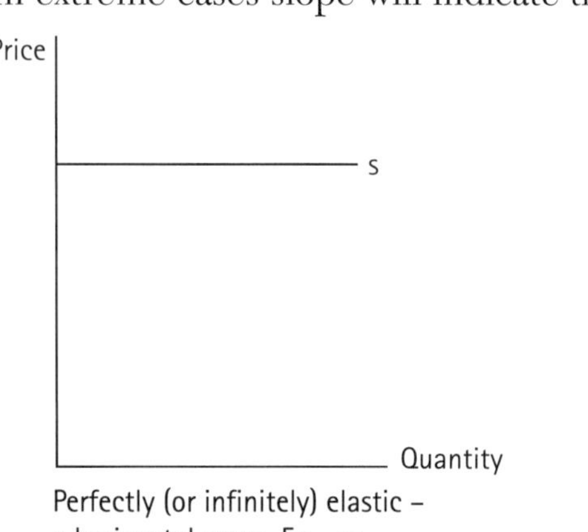

Perfectly (or infinitely) elastic – a horizontal curve, Es = ∞

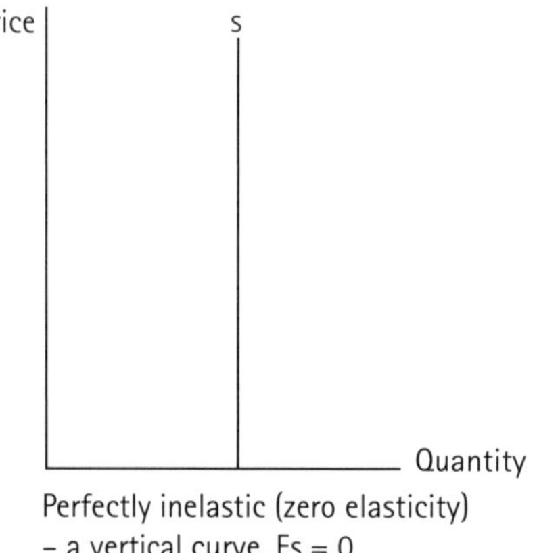

Perfectly inelastic (zero elasticity) – a vertical curve, Es = 0

ISBN 9780170241212

Inelastic and elastic supply

When price elasticity of supply is less than one this means that a given change in price causes a less than proportionate change in quantity supplied and indicates inelastic supply.

When price elasticity of supply is greater than one this means that a given change in price causes a more than proportionate change in quantity supplied and indicates elastic supply.

Supply over time

Supply is inelastic, or relatively unresponsive to price changes in the short run, and elastic, or relatively responsive, in the long run.

In the **short-run time period**, at least one input is fixed. The firm is restricted in its ability to change output. In the short run the supply of all goods is inelastic because the quantity supplied is limited to the quantity of finished goods on hand or easily available. Supply elasticity is said to be lower.

In the **long run** firms have time to expand their use of *all* factors and so increase their total output capacity. Shortages and profits will attract more firms to the industry, which will increase total market supply. Over time, supply will be more responsive to price (elastic) as existing producers are able to increase production levels, new producers can enter the market, and improvements in technology increase productivity. Elasticity is then said to be higher.

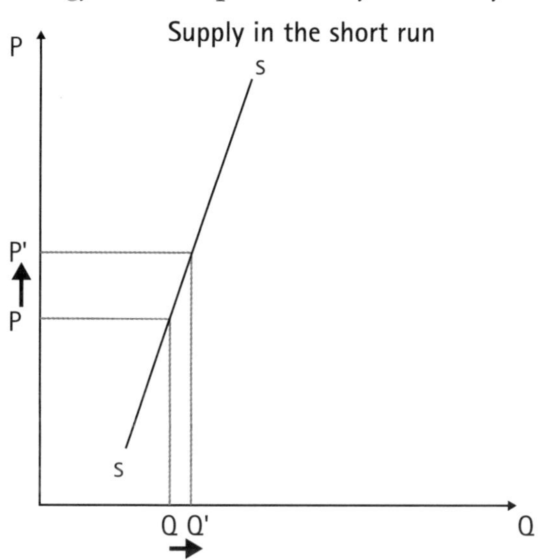

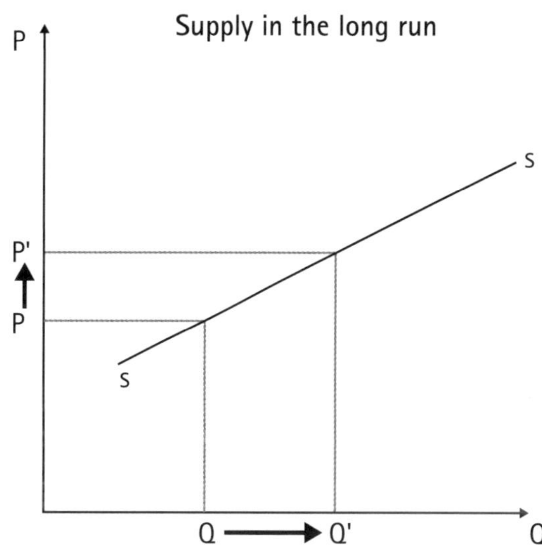

In response to a price change output will change by more in the long-run than short-run time period, as shown in the two diagrams.

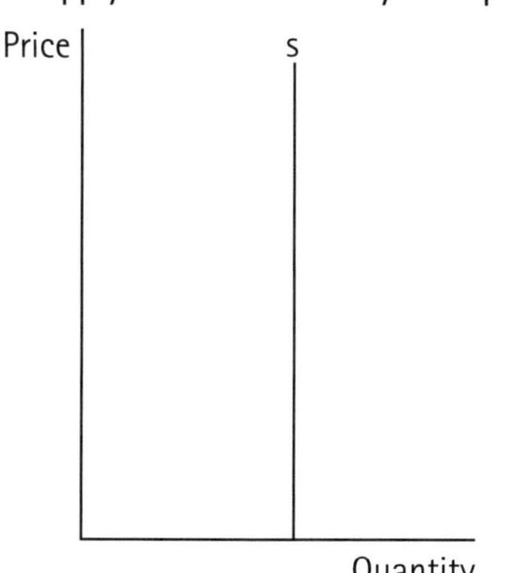

Momentary supply is supply at this moment in time and is sometimes referred to as supply on a given day when quantity supplied is fixed regardless of price.

This is illustrated by the perfectly inelastic supply curve shown, drawn as a vertical line.

The curve reflects that firms have only a fixed amount of stock on hand available to meet demand and are unable to alter any factors, for example tickets to a school social, or the lots available for sale at an auction.

There is no responsiveness in the quantity supplied to a change in price and the coefficient of elasticity of supply is zero.

ISBN 9780170241212

Key terms and ideas

Price elasticity of supply (Es)	Measures the responsiveness of quantity supplied of a good to changes in its price
Formula to calculate price elasticity of supply, midpoint method Es > 1, elastic Es = 1, unitary Es < 1, inelastic	$$Es = \frac{\left(\dfrac{\text{change in quantity supplied}}{\text{midpoint of quantity supplied given}}\right)}{\left(\dfrac{\text{change in price}}{\text{midpoint of the prices indicated}}\right)} = \frac{\left(\dfrac{\Delta Qs}{\frac{Q1 + Q2}{2}}\right)}{\left(\dfrac{\Delta P}{\frac{P1 + P2}{2}}\right)}$$
Inelastic supply (Es < 1)	A given change in price causes a less than proportionate change in quantity supplied.
Elastic supply (Es > 1)	A given change in price causes a more than proportionate change in quantity supplied.
Momentary time period (or supply on a given day) 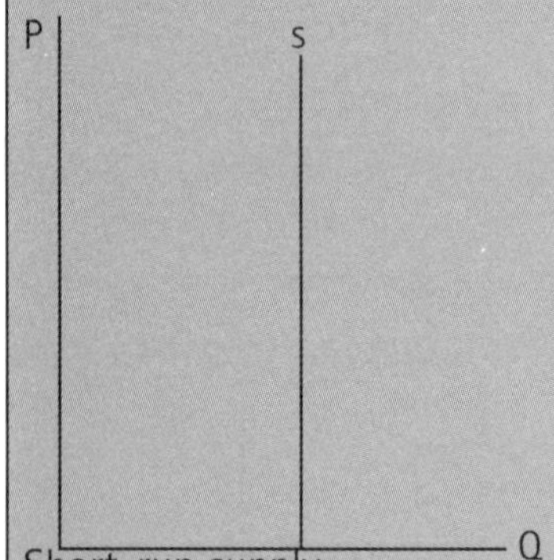 P S Q	The quantity supplied is fixed and cannot respond to changes in price; the curve is drawn as a vertical line and is perfectly inelastic. Firms are unable to change any inputs (factors).
Short-run supply 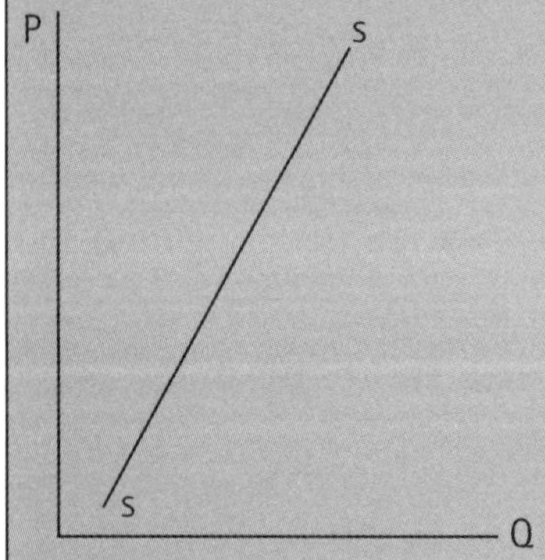 P S S Q	At least one input is fixed and therefore the firm is restricted in its ability to change supply/output levels. Supply in the short run will be more inelastic (or lower) and less elastic.
Long-run supply 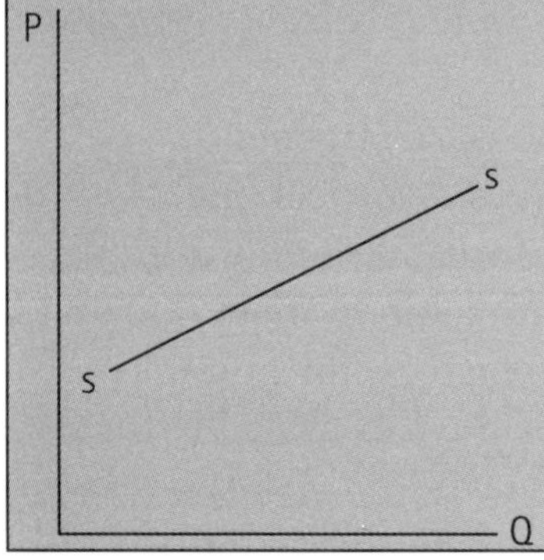 P S S Q	All inputs are variable therefore the firm can be more adaptable and more efficient. Supply is more elastic (or higher) and less inelastic in the long run.

ISBN 9780170241212

Student notes: Price elasticity of supply, Es

ISBN 9780170241212

Practise questions and tasks

1 a Define 'price elasticity of supply'.

b Work out the price elasticity of supply for each question below (show your working). Use the midpoint method.

(i)

Price ($)	Quantity supplied
1.00	17
0.95	10

(ii)

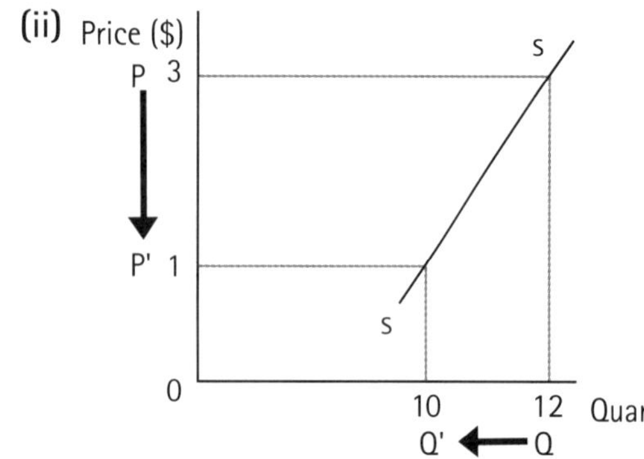

c Use the diagram to match up the curves with the description below. Write the letter of your choice.

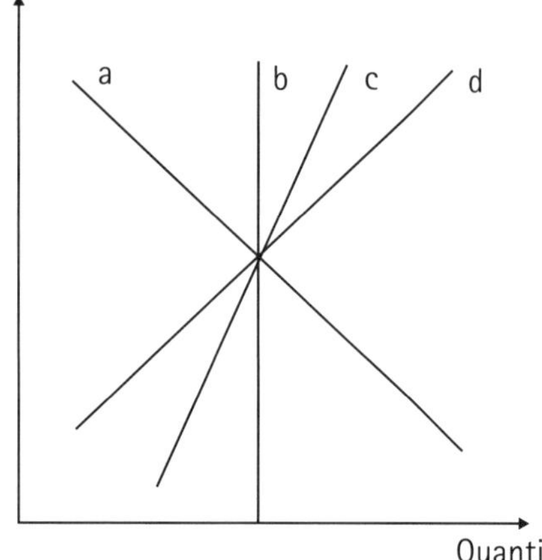

Relatively inelastic supply

Demand curve

Momentary supply curve – on a given day

Relatively elastic supply

d Describe the price elasticity of supply indicated by the situations outlined in the table below.

Situation	Elasticity
(i) The response to a given change in price is a more than proportionate change in quantity supplied.	
(ii) The response to a given change in price is a less than proportionate change in quantity supplied.	
(iii) A given price change causes no change in quantity supplied.	
(iv) %Δ price > %Δ quantity supplied	
(v) %Δ quantity supplied > %Δ price	

ISBN 9780170241212

2 Calculate the price elasticity of supply for each question below (show your working). Use the midpoint method.

a

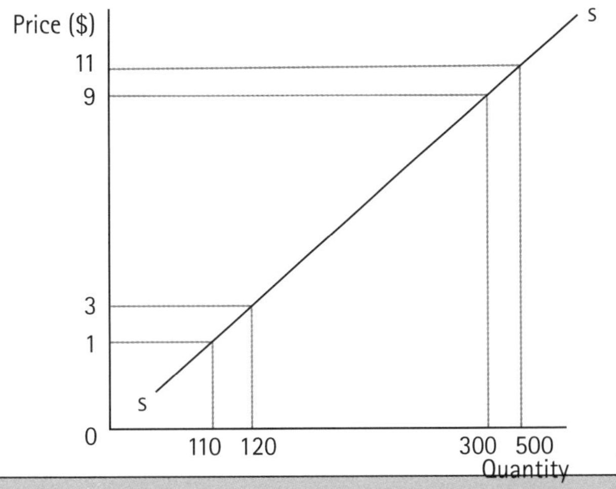

(i) Between $11 and $9:

(ii) Between $3 and $1:

b Briefly explain why there is a difference in the short-run and long-run supply curves for bottled water.

c What is the price elasticity of supply when quantity supplied increases from 10 to 12 as the price increases from $200 to $250? Show your working.

d Define 'supply elasticity' and give the formula to calculate Es.

ISBN 9780170241212

3 Below are the correct supply curves in the short-run and long-run time periods. Use these graphs and your own knowledge to complete the sentences that follow.

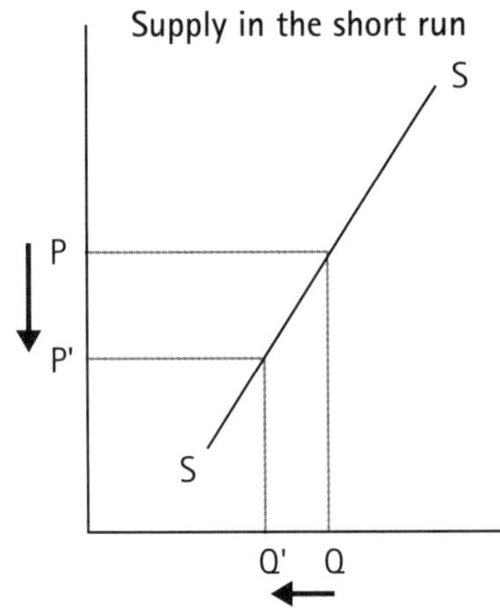

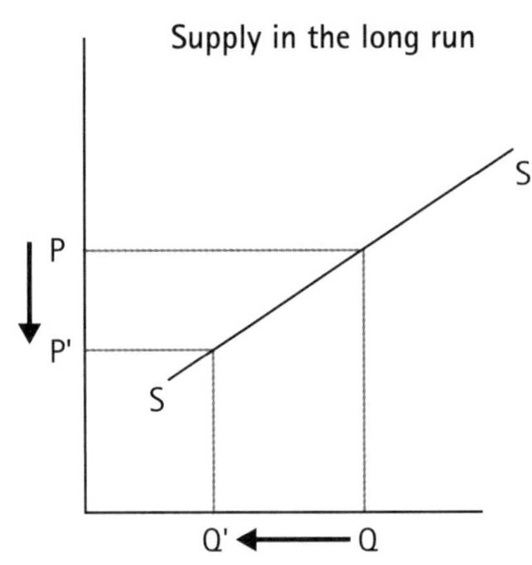

a Supply in the short run is relatively ______________ and in the long run relatively ______________.

b 'In response to a price d______________ the output will fall by more in the ______________ run than it does in the ______________ run.'

c In the short run supply is relatively unr______________ and in the long run more r______________.

d Supply on a given day is p______________ i______________ and the curve is drawn as a ______________ line.

e When a given price change causes a more than proportionate change in quantity supplied this indicates ______________. The short-run supply curve is relatively i______________.

f Inelastic supply occurs when a given change ______________ ______________. The long-run supply is relatively e______________.

4 Calculate price elasticity of supply for each question below (show your working). Use the midpoint method.

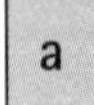

a

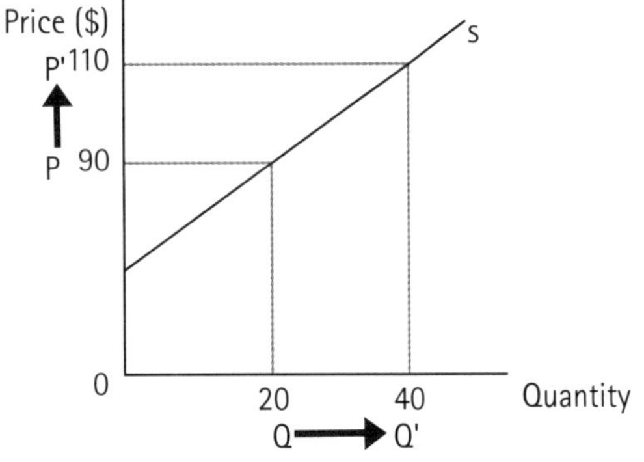

____

____

b

Price ($)	Quantity supplied
1.00	30
1.50	34

____

____

ISBN 9780170241212

Review questions

1 Supply over time

Supply is inelastic, or relatively unresponsive to price changes in the short run, and elastic, or relatively responsive, in the long run.

Explain supply over time. In your answer you should use diagrams and:

- Explain the momentary time period.
- Explain the short-run time period.
- Explain the long-run time period.

ISBN 9780170241212

2 Alfred Marshall developed the economic theory that price elasticity of supply for a good or service is linked to time periods.

Graph 1: The Market Supply of Fish

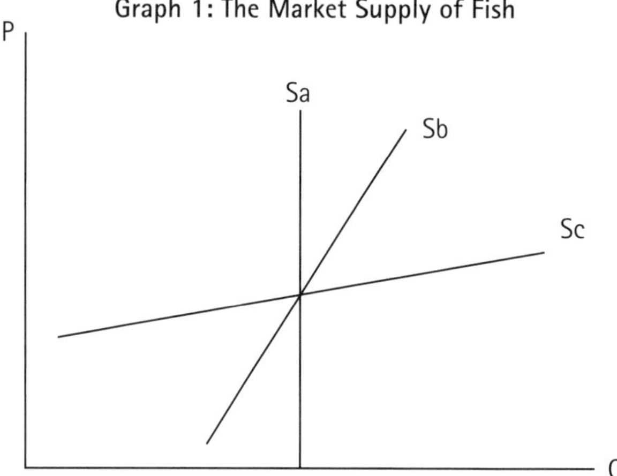

Explain price elasticity of supply. In your answer you should:

- Define price elasticity of supply and explain the difference between inelastic and elastic supply.
- Assume that fish prices have increased. With reference to Graph 1, explain which of the three supply curves for fish is most appropriate for a period of one year. Justify your answer.

SELF-EVALUATION REVIEW

Tick (✔) which of the following you know the precise economic answers to (go back and learn those that you have not ticked).

	(✔) TICK
Define 'price elasticity of supply'.	☐
Calculate price elasticity of supply.	☐
Explain why supply is more responsive in the long run than in the short run.	☐
Apply the concept of elasticity of supply in a given situation.	☐

ISBN 9780170241212

ROLE OF PRICES AND PROFITS

Key concepts and terms: sunrise and sunset industries (3.3).

SUNRISE AND SUNSET INDUSTRIES

A firm is a single business while an industry is the sum of all firms which produce one type of product. The dairy industry in New Zealand includes all those firms involved in producing dairy products for sale from the farmers who milk cows, firms who process the milk into final or intermediate products, and firms who market the final product.

If prices for dairy products in world markets rise, the industry as a whole will prosper and grow. Dairy farmers will be encouraged to invest more in milk production. For example, farmers may purchase land, converting sheep farms to dairy production. This will involve the purchase of capital items such as milking sheds, tractors and equipment. Milk production will increase, farmers' incomes will rise and they may employ extra workers.

Factories processing milk and firms marketing the final product will also increase output and sales. Employment will rise and spending will increase beyond the dairy industry.

The hospitality and travel industry may well benefit as individuals with increased disposable incomes take holidays and travel. Regions whose economies are dependent on the dairy industry are likely to benefit the most from the expansion in economic activity.

As domestic and global economies go through the trade cycle of recession, recovery and boom, it is likely that the part of the trade cycle that the New Zealand economy is in will differ from a number of its trading partners. If there is a downturn in overseas demand, there are likely to be reduced incomes and possibly business closures for firms that rely heavily on export orders. Unemployment is likely to rise and living standards in the affected areas and communities will be lower.

The converse applies for a recovery and increase in overseas demand. While some industries may be experiencing a decline in activities it is possible that other industries are experiencing growth, e.g., while the car and shoe manufacturing industries have declined, other industries such as tourism, wine, education and dairying have grown in size and importance in the New Zealand economy.

The changing demand for a product in local or world markets may be temporary or permanent. Resources will switch from declining industries (**sunset**) into growth industries (**sunrise**) where prospects and profits are likely to be better.

There is always likely to be a change in the fortune of various industries within an economy at any given point in time. The change will mean some individuals losing jobs in some industries, while new opportunities arise in other industries, some firms' profits declining while others are growing, firms may close down or may go through a process of restructuring.

KEY TERMS AND IDEAS

Firm	A single business.
Industry	The sum of all firms which produce one type of product.
Sunrise industry	A growth (expanding) industry where prospects and profits are likely to be improving.
Sunset industry	A declining industry where resources will be shifted away into other industries where their prospects are better and the returns to the owners are higher.

ISBN 9780170241212

Student notes: Role of prices and profits

ISBN 9780170241212

PRACTISE QUESTIONS AND TASKS

Government economic reform and changes in domestic and international demand patterns have transformed the New Zealand economy. Businesses have shifted from old 'sunset' industries to innovative 'sunrise' industries.

1 a Indicate if the following industries are 'sunset' or 'sunrise' industries.

(i)	boat building	______	(ii)	organics	______
(iii)	car manufacturing	______	(iv)	wine	______
(v)	education	______	(vi)	tourism	______
(vii)	film making	______	(viii)	shoe manufacturing	______
(ix)	dairying	______	(x)	wool and sheep	______

b The difficulty with economic reform is the short-term losses, and long-run gains. Outline some possible short-term losses and long-run gains that were a result of from reform policies that liberalised trade in New Zealand.

(i) Short-term losses: ______

______

______

(ii) Long-term gains: ______

______

______

c Indicate if the following statements are facts or opinions. Justify your answers.

(i) A 'sunset' industry will always be a 'sunset' industry. ______

______

______

______

(ii) The growth and contraction of some New Zealand industries will depend on what goes on in the global economy. ______

______

______

______

______

______

______

ISBN 9780170241212

2 a (i) Complete the table to indicate if the following event or situation will result in growth or contraction of industries.

(ii) Complete the table with a tick (✓) to indicate which industries are likely to be affected by the situation or event outlined.

Situation or event	Growth or contraction of industries	Education industry	Tourism industry	Marine industry	Farming (agriculture/ horticulture) industry
New Zealand wins the Americas Cup.					
An outbreak of mad cow disease in Europe and America.					
A SARS outbreak in Asia and downturn in Asian economies.					
A reduction in quotas and tariffs on New Zealand-made products by the European Union.					

b Complete the table with a tick (✓) to indicate if the situation outlined is likely to occur when the economy is expanding or contracting.

Situation	Expanding economy	Contracting economy
(i) A rise in the number of business closures.		
(ii) A decrease in the number of building consents.		
(iii) An increase in the level of business confidence.		
(iv) Workers are being made redundant and levels of unemployment are rising.		
(v) Firms are paying workers overtime and there is a scarcity of resources available.		
(vi) Increased investment by firms and Real GDP is rising.		
(vii) Firms are recording record sales and company profits rise.		

c Complete the statements below using the words provided.

consumer	dying	growth	restructured	sunset
declining	dynamic	losing	retrain	Workers
down	expanding	prospects	sunrise	

Markets are ____________, they are constantly changing as a result of changes in ____________ tastes and preferences. ____________ who lose jobs in ____________ industries may need to ____________ in skills demanded by the expanding (____________) industries. Resources should reallocate from ____________ or ____________ industries (sunset) to ____________ or ____________ industries (sunrise) where ____________ are better. The change from sunset to sunrise industries will mean some individuals ____________ jobs, firms closing ____________ or being ____________.

ISBN 9780170241212

3 Read the extract and answer the questions that follow.

> An outbreak of mad cow disease in Europe is predicted to have an impact on the level of economic activity in New Zealand immediately and in the long term. Recent years have seen an increase in global demand for agricultural product.

a List several economic effects on the New Zealand farming industry of mad cow disease in Europe.

b Identify the likely impact on economic growth in New Zealand indicated by the information in the extract.

c Suggest one possible reason for the 'increasing global demand for agricultural products'.

d Describe what happens in an industry when the industry expands.

e Explain the effect of the dairy industry success on New Zealand's dairy regions.

ISBN 9780170241212

Review questions

1 The ski industry continues to grow as more tourists visit during the New Zealand winter. Explain the impact of the ski industry on the New Zealand economy. In your answer you should:

- Explain the effect of increased tourist numbers on the ski industry in New Zealand.
- Explain the effect on prices and profit.

ISBN 9780170241212

2 Foreign fee-paying student numbers continue to decline as the recession continues and the dollar appreciates.

Explain, using the education industry, the effect on an industry when it is in decline. In your answer you should:

- Explain the effect on providers of education.
- Explain the flow-on effects to other industries, profits and resource use.

SELF-EVALUATION REVIEW

Tick (✔) which of the following you know the precise economic answers to (go back and learn those that you have not ticked).

	(✔) TICK
Explain the role of prices and profits.	☐

ISBN 9780170241212

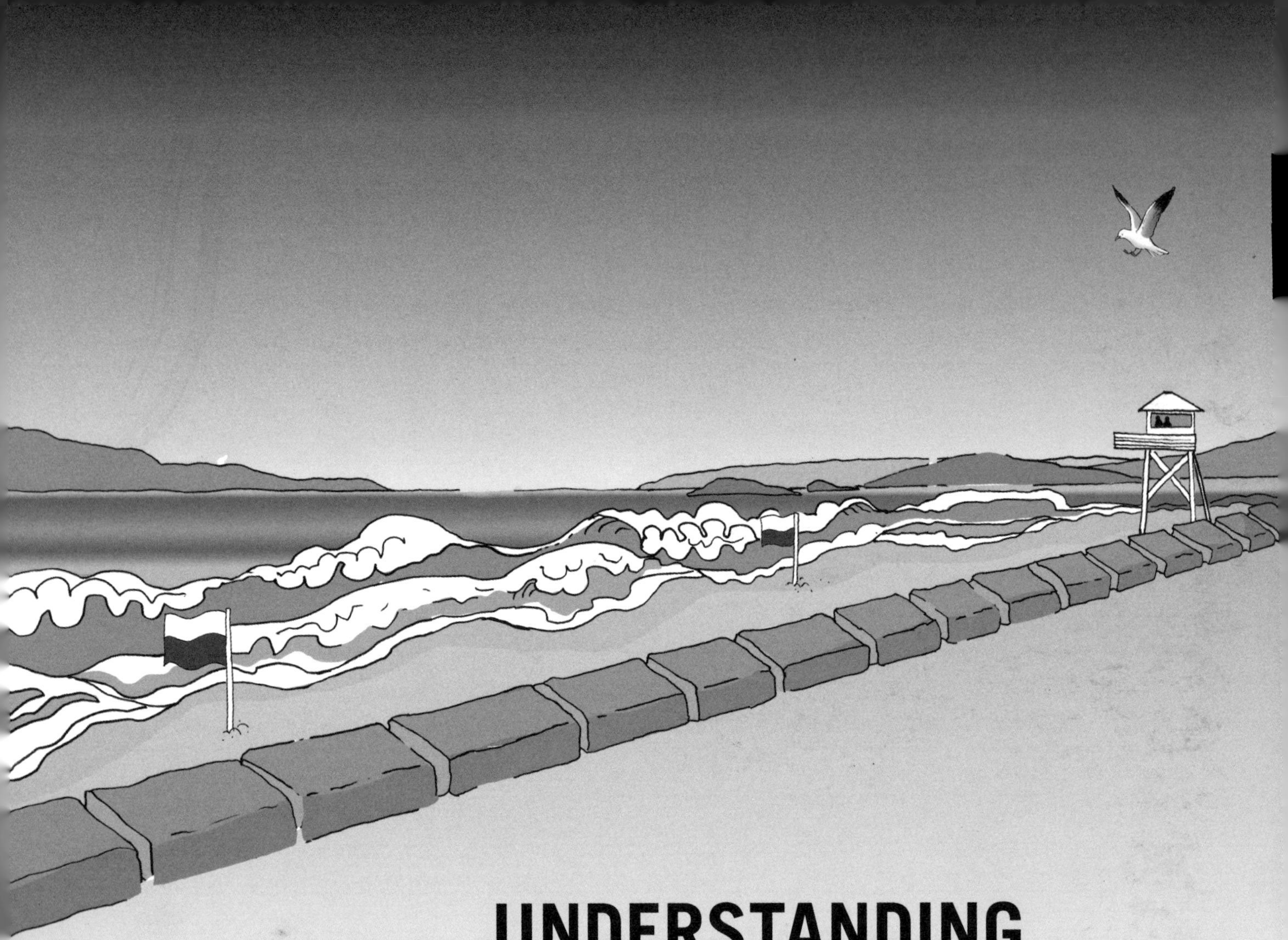

UNDERSTANDING ECONOMICS

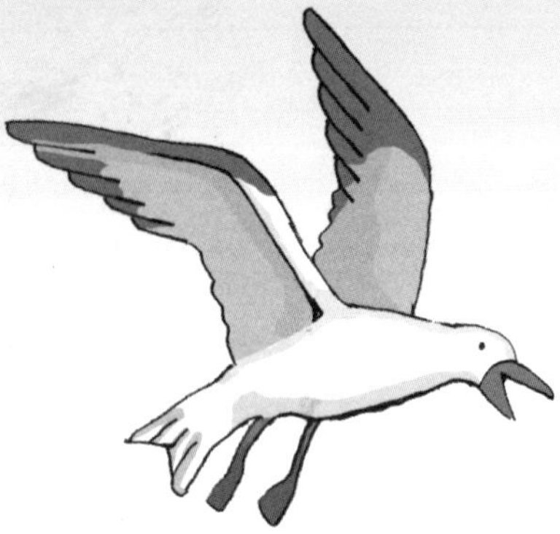

For NCEA Level THREE | INTERNAL | MICRO-ECONOMIC CONCEPTS is a self contained textbook/workbook designed to satisfy the requirements of the recent curriculum changes and allow students to develop the Key Competencies with a range of learning activities.

Concise notes and a comprehensive set of activities work to introduce and develop the Economic definitions, concepts and skills students require for the Internal Achievement Standard: Demonstrate understanding of micro-economic concepts. Review questions in each chapter allow students an opportunity to test their understanding and prepare for an internal standard.

Notes and activities in this book have been trialled with NCEA Level Three classes in Economics over several years with excellent results.

For learning solutions, visit **cengage.com.au**

ISBN 978-0170241212

9 780170 241212